Contents

Ways of Being a Body

Published in this first edition in 2013 by:
Triarchy Press
Station Offices
Axminster
Devon. EX13 5PF
United Kingdom

+44 (0)1297 631456
info@triarchypress.com
www.triarchypress.net

A catalogue record for this book is available from the British Library.

Front cover painting by Greta Berlin.
www.gretaberlin.co.uk

ISBN:978-1-909470-16-3

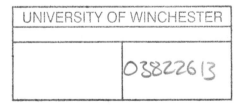

INTRODUCTION

The first volume in this series, *Nine Ways of Seeing a Body*, offered a historical perspective on different key approaches to the body over time. This new edited collection brings to light a wide range of contemporary approaches to the body that are currently being used by performers or in the context of performance training.

Body and Performance brings together twelve 'lenses' that are specifically connected to a praxis of the body in performance. A 'lens' is defined here as a way of seeing, thinking about and engaging with the body as well as articulating and theorising that experience.

The various lenses offered here all reject the notion of treating the 'body as object'. Instead of trying to improve or enhance the body, they support the individual as a creative entity, as a 'being.becoming.being'. They share both a respect for the unknown as a part of their enquiry and a commitment to researching the psychophysical body within the field of performance. They place attention on where the practitioner 'comes from' in movement rather than on what technique(s) the body can be made to undergo or execute.

Each lens prioritises different aspects of the experience of a co-creative interaction between self and others and between self and the environment. A wealth of information and exploratory material is generated by setting these different views alongside one another, stimulating in me the desire for further debate as well as allowing new thoughts and possible ways of working to emerge from the spaces inbetween the various practices.

In their descriptive analysis of the different 'bodies', these 12 lenses also share a commitment to 'being present and in presence'.

From different angles and in varying degrees these chapters all examine one or more of the following themes: the body as process (have a look at The Ontogenetic Body), place as process (The Dwelling Body) and, in various ways, the mutual interdependence of body and place (The Dwelling

Body, The Learnt Body, The Inter-subjective Body, The Resonant Body and The Autobiographical Body).

Some chapters examine material generated from the body-mind through improvisation, as seen through the lenses of inter-subjectivity, autobiography (of a collective and relational kind) and resonance. The Cognitive Body explores the mechanism of embodied selection, faced with a wealth of creative material generated through improvisation.

The Vocal Body challenges an essentialist view of voice and vocal training and The Musical Body challenges both the habitual divorce of the body from the musical statement and the notion of the body as a functional adjunct to the production of music. Both of these chapters offer welcome material for students of the performing arts to consider carefully.

Some chapters explore the nature of physiological habits and how these can be challenged and dissolved through different somatic approaches – for example Feldenkrais (The Resilient Body), the Alexander Technique (The Imaginal Body) and Body-Mind Centering (The Inter-subjective Body and The Ontogenetic Body).

Questions and qualities of temporality are implicit in any movement-based research – rhythm, diachronic time (time seen as duration) and synchronic time (time seen as separate moments) to name but three. In particular, the word 'habit' referred to above implies a fixed relationship to time and flow, one that can be accepted, satisfied, disrupted and transformed through the dynamics of a body in movement. An awareness of temporality in relation to the body means that a 'pattern' does not have to remain forever fixed. A fixed notion of time is just one part of a fixed notion of self.

Among the chapters in this collection, The Kinetic Body explores time and rhythm explicitly, looking at how, within the performance tradition of *Kudiyattam*, "the foot positions and pathways render the collective ceremony of the bodily re-collections" and how, through the motion of foot, "the symbolic world of performance unfolds in the spectacle of the body".

This consideration of the relationship between what may be called the 'world of fact' (for example the sensed and sensuous physicality of the body) and the 'world of dream'[1] (the symbolic or imaginal world) is woven into the very fabric of performance. In connection with their audiences, for the duration of a situated moment, bodies create and recreate stories; they create space, time and characters (or modes) that co-exist in the world of fact and in the world of dream. This is part of the magic of the collective shared experience of live performance.

Once again, this collection of lenses and the application of various somatic approaches is by no means exhaustive. The intention is for practitioners, teachers and students of the performing arts as well as directors or choreographers to locate their own preferred approach(es) and lenses amongst those described here and to explore those alternatives that might enrich their vocabulary.

The next collection in this series (following a similar format) will address approaches to body and awareness. If you have a response to the lenses presented in the present book or would like to contribute to the next one, please feel free to send me your ideas, suggestions or writings.

Sandra Reeve – June 2013

Dr. Sandra Reeve is a movement teacher, artist, director and movement psychotherapist, offering therapy and supervision in private practice. Since 1999, she has taught an annual programme of autobiographical and environmental movement workshops called Move into Life and she creates occasional, small-scale ecological performances.

She is an Honorary Fellow at the University of Exeter, specialising in Performance and Ecology.
www.moveintolife.com
sandra@moveintolife.co.uk

---

1   'World of fact' and 'world of dream' are terms used in *Joged Amerta*, a somatic and performance practice developed by Suprapto Suryodarmo, Javanese movement artist and teacher. www.lemahputih.com

The Ontogenetic Body

An Exploration Based on Body-Mind Centering

Róisín O'Gorman

Abstract

ONTOGENESIS[1] describes the developmental journey from our embryonic forms towards our full maturity. This chapter offers an experiential and reflective account of working with an ontogenetic approach to embodied movement practices for performance, with particular focus on material drawn from BODY-MIND CENTERING (BMC).

Grounded in ethnographic examples, the chapter demonstrates that through BMC, a conscious, playful re-encountering of our ontogenesis renews and expands our movement vocabularies and our perceptual ranges; it allows us to shift or expand our sense of subjectivity. Each example offers momentary reflections on particular aspects of the ontogenetic body, showing how the ontogenetic experience shifts our perceptions and hurls us into a confrontation with the unknown and unknowable of human existence and evolution.

It also provokes many, more tangible questions, for example: What happens if we consciously embody our earliest cellular forms and the movement vocabularies that shaped our earliest explorations of our worlds? What might we understand of performance and pregnancy, of movement and creativity if we open a mind's eye to textures, sensations and cognition from the ontogenetic body's point of view?

The ontogenetic body is a way of moving and a mode of perception. It makes us aware of developmental processes and gives us a method for embodying the forms, mind states and movement patterns of our cellular histories. This can challenge the ways in which we see every body and opens our eyes to our interconnections and inter-vulnerabilities.

---

1   All terms listed in the Glossary appear, as here, in small capitals the first time they are mentioned in each chapter.

Ontogenesis: A moving place, sometimes of origin, a place of spaces, of being becoming and unbecoming, of structures becoming and coming undone, not uni-linear but interwoven layers, generative, inter-generational, multi-directional, multi-dimensional, patterning in time, through selves.

Yolk Sacs and Amniotic cavities: an exploration

...tiny... starting out... setting up house ...embryonic

J and I begin our exploration by looking at Bonnie Bainbridge Cohen's drawings of the embryo in development and how we fold around and 'swallow' the yolk sac. This sac is like an embryonic 'snack pack' that nourishes the embryo in the first weeks of development. It forms to the front side of what will become the body, to the back the amniotic cavity develops, ultimately providing baby with a swimming space.[2]

We play with large gym balls – one to the front of the body, one to the back of the body. We each have the balls buoyantly supporting front and back. We wedge and wiggle ourselves between them against the wall and the floor and in corners. This allows for a funny floating feeling, a dangling that is supported, a form that is free. We play warm samba music and we find buoyant joy, a bounce and rebound in the built structures transferring supporting weight.

...light ... dancing ... joy
Joy   Laughter Joy Joy

It gives us an intimation of a gravity-free sensation.

Joy: we are tickled by this buoyancy. We laugh. J sneezes, releasing.

Joy: we then play together, holding and rolling the balls, helping each other to feel what it is like to have support to both the front and back of the body; to float, roll, dive, fly in the in-between spaces and then letting those sensations come inwards.

We feel the pressure and release into it – being squeezed can be a support! We draw, we write, we laugh, we talk it over, and then we go and eat some delicious

---

2   This exploration is based on the interview 'The Place of Space' in Bainbridge Cohen (2008). Please refer to this for a detailed explanation of these terms and explorations.

things. The curious bubbling feelings support us; our buoyancy comes alive, reflated. We learn that we carry our support in ourselves first and foremost, but that a friend can also help us bounce back.

Joy
Joy Joy Joy

What is ontogenesis?

The ontogenetic body is the conscious embodiment of ontogenesis. Ontogenesis describes the developmental journey from our embryonic forms towards our full maturity. Body-Mind Centering (BMC) offers myriad practices for embodying this formative experience: through touch, movement, sound, play, imagination and observation. By paying particular attention to our earliest states of being and becoming, BMC maps the embodiment of ontogenetic (human) and phylogenetic (animal) patterns of movement and development. The maps created and explored are cartographies of being; charting internal landscapes and moving structures, they offer many movement pathways. Some may be familiar; others less so. As movers work with this material, they often realise that these patterns have been there all along; with conscious awareness and embodiment of their ontogenetic patterns, they discover new ways of building vocabulary and they experience new articulations and deeper resonances even within very familiar movement practices.

Thinking through and creating with the ontogenetic body is useful in any number of settings from performance practices and creative work to therapeutic situations.[3] This essay uses ethnographic vignettes to present some examples and descriptions of embodied ontogenetic explorations.[4]

---

3   This essay focuses more particularly on performance-related situations. For a therapeutic approach see Linda Hartley (1995), in particular her chapter on 'Developmental Movement Therapy'. However, the two areas are fundamentally related as Hartley explains: "We find that this re-education of underlying developmental patterns [through Developmental Movement Therapy] not only gives more inner strength, clarity, and aliveness to our movement and percep-tual responses, but it also frees more of our energy for creative thought and activity." (p.91)

4   The reflections in this essay are based on my encounters with BMC in courses taken with Margie Fargnoli at the University of Minnesota and with the Embody-Move Association in the UK as well as individual explorations and group sessions I have led with theatre students and performance practitioners.

The italic sections interspersed throughout this chapter detail three varied threads of experiential ontogenesis. The first, above, offers an exploration with a choreographer based on BMC's attention to embryonic structures; the next truncates a series of workshops with a film maker which formed the basis for DEVISING a new project; the third thread describes my own experience of being pregnant.[5]

While disparate, each example reaches for a moment of free-fall, of a dropping-into awareness and presence, of finding openings to free oneself from habitual choices or patterns, to allow space for the paradoxes and complexities of lived experiences and to find ways of opening to creative possibilities. All together they represent a scene of creativity, which ultimately – in both literal and figurative terms – is a birthing: of oneself, of another, of a work, of a world. Pregnancy and performance offer two tangible sites for exploring this ontology. Both exemplify subjectivity in flux as the mother-baby body and the performer-role body vibrate with multiplicities and refuse to remain still. Through BMC, a conscious, playful re-encountering of our ontogenesis renews and expands our movement vocabularies and our perceptual ranges; it allows us to shift or expand our sense of subjectivity. These examples also underscore the way in which movement development happens in overlapping waves, where transitions are not always smooth or easy, where a leap forwards can be surprising and where we might wonder what propels us to the next stage or what draws us back to an earlier impulse or pattern we thought we were done with.

It is not possible to be comprehensive in this short chapter; instead I aim to evoke at least some sense of the lived experience of ontogenesis, to point to possibilities for future explorations, to consider what is possible when we access the ontology of our ontogeny, and further to consider how this relates to performance. The sections offer momentary reflections on particular aspects of the ontogenetic body, with the intention of allowing an open and overlapping intermingling of sites and thoughts rather than any promise of a completed, hermetic, knowable object. Instead, the ontogenetic experience shifts our perceptions and can hurl us into a confrontation with the unknown and unknowable of human existence and evolution. It also provokes many questions that are (somewhat) more

---

5   Following ethnographic convention, the subject's name is not used.

tangible, for example: What happens if we consciously embody our earliest cellular forms and the movement vocabularies that shaped our earliest explorations of our worlds? What might we understand of performance and pregnancy, of movement and creativity if we open a mind's eye to textures, sensations and cognition from the ontogenetic body's point of view?

Cellular life: From the beginning we are two and from there we are multiple

> "To begin, the egg and sperm unite. What's exciting is that it used to be thought that from the union of the egg and the sperm you have a primary cell that divides and duplicates. But it turns out that the first cell is two cells. ...The first cell is two. I love that. We are communicating already; we have different polarities immediately. We are always two. Isn't that fascinating?" (Bainbridge Cohen, 2008: 164)

In the midst of debates on the contested science and ethics of stem cell research and the politics of reproduction, BMC more quietly and delicately enables anyone to explore an embodied experience of their own cellular experiences, when we were but a beginning, a barely there, a cluster of cells.

In recent years Bainbridge Cohen has researched aspects of human formation at a detailed embryological level, searching for the vestigial support of embryonic structures. She describes this stage in her work as moving from embodying structure (through a cellular awareness) to an embodying of space through "embryological structures that don't exist any more but whose processes still inform us" (*ibid*: 167). In the exploration described above we played as a way to magnify the embryonic structures to a larger external world and followed the opening impulses from there.

This exploration generated a framework of questions which I continue to explore. For example: what does it feel like to embody space? What are the spaces we embody internally? How does embodying space shift the mind? What potential is here for performers to increase their expressive range and to understand and shift habitual patterns? How do I experience internal support and patterning and how does that experience shape my relationships with the external environment and with others? How does this process operate in performance?

Performing Past

M and I enter the studio. We are working together on a performance project about memories, legacies and dreaming. We look for a way into the world of the piece; we move to find a beginning, a shared language and feeling, a place to start building a project out of the woven, fragmented stories of our ancestral lines. We wonder about how those bodies carried our bodies and what information, genetic or otherwise, we now carry, knowing or unknowing. What can be remembered? What is evoked, provoked, conjured in our tissues? What does our genetic code reveal and conceal? How can we tap this replenishing resource? We play some music and begin to move separately in the space.

As we move, my focus is on the ontogenetic body and what it might offer us as a way into memory and imagination. In this way the ontogenetic body can be a site of discovery of movement and images for devising work. The patterns are pre-verbal and as M drops into the work I feel the chattering mind quietening. M has a lot of energy and needs to move. His head, however, seems to be held at a distance so I make suggestions to move from the navel, to embody the starfish pattern of navel radiation. He allows the navel to become the organising centre of movement, all limbs become equal including the head and the tail. His head releases, engages. We continue to move. We feel the flow of pulsation and sponging, two early transitional patterns that shape the body as it is moved by the flow of the environment in and around itself. Moving through these patterns the gut becomes very present and allows for a certain directionality to enter, a quiet verticality emerges through a clear sense of top and tail, of beginning and ending, of reaching out and pulling into oneself, opening and closing, defending and desiring. The patterns interweave in any one moment and movement, each one supporting the next.

The ontogenetic subject is alive to performance as a mode that works to access the fluidity of creativity. In this way performance practices can offer us methods to enter the ontogenetic body and vice versa. The session described above formed part of devising a new work incorporating film into live performance. I became the film actor, which was a new experience for me. The movement explorations we shared together were part of the ongoing work in developing the project, allowing a shared understanding of a feeling, an atmosphere, and a potentiality that we tapped into in generating filmic material both outdoors and in studio settings. As a performer I felt that the presence and intensity of camera work was supported by the awareness brought about by the ontogenetic body. This awareness supported an open vulnerability, giving structure and choice to follow impulses and respond to the environment, objects and the presence of the camera.

The ontogenetic body, then, is a relational body, one continually experiencing its own becoming within a temporal and moving environment. This awareness can support a performer to find ways of opening to a certain vulnerability and presence, helping to create pathways to express and externalise internal experiences and to find support in the external environment for their internal work.

Infancy

M is in his own movement; suddenly he opens his eyes, a kind of contact. Now he has gone foetal, and without prompting he begins moving between full body flexion and extension. I support this with a hand on his sacrum and another to the back of his head helping him to engage and connect through the c-curve of his body. I move to his feet and give as strong a grounded support as I can; against this resistance he launches into the whole room.

Later we write and draw and talk. We continue to wonder at the links and influences of our grandparents and other progenitors and if we are trying to tell their story or ours. If we are creating a ghost story in this dream piece (how) are we haunted by our genetic demons? M has gathered some fragments of stories and some archival material – a letter, some photographs. It is, however, through these bodies/body-minds that the portal between these worlds is opened and explored, where history and imagination are both contained and expressed, where they linger and dissolve.

I did not speak in this project and in its first public performance there was no traditional text; instead we had a movement, sound and visual score. It is still a work in progress. As I continue to explore the ontogenetic body, one of the ongoing challenges is how to integrate this work with the voice – whether and how one can speak from this place. This involves the fundamental hook between sound and movement, allowing the voice to move and movement to speak.

Infant means one without language (etymologically, it derives from the Latin *infantia or* inability to speak). To return to these patterns from infancy as an adult can challenge our verbal and cognitive habits. While verbal instruction and description are useful, it is also worth letting go of the too-often linear drive of language and to explore instead the playful possibilities of one's voice and sound-making. In playing with and discovering the ontogenetic patterns it can be helpful to explore voice itself as a movement response, a motoring into the world, a free form of movement that children (usually) know how to explore endlessly. As in the best performances and most vital experiences, in the ontogenetic body, language interweaves with laughter and imagination, exudes beyond representation into the pulsating and vibrating spaces around words and sounds; words gasp and flesh into world, and the world whorls into flesh, and maybe, through performance, we can speak from there.

Liken me to lichens

As my body grew in pregnancy I became more than one but not yet two. I struggled to find a way to describe my experience. Yes, there was a baby inside my body, but he was growing, dancing and developing with me, through me, as me and not as me and my me also moved into new territories of form and identities.

For this window of time we are as one, as you are not yet you but still more than part of me.

When I'm about six months pregnant we go on a forest walk hunting mushrooms. We are lucky to be led by a savvy mycologist ensuring we don't poison ourselves. We learn about the intricate hidden networks of fungi under the huge old trees around us. We are no longer just tramping through the woods but our senses are re-calibrated. The world shifts, my sense of smell, already heightened in pregnancy, registers the damp fecundity, in the dim light I feel like I'm smelling through my eyes. As with BMC, with the right guide and re-tuned awareness we start to see what has been there all along, in this case the tiny creatures bursting out in the half light under and on the trees. As we go deeper into the woods the mycologist also points out the various lichens texturing the scene. She explains the structure of a lichen as part fungi and part algae, coming together to create this hybrid yet unique entity. Something clicks inside me. For a while the metaphor fits, and I need a metaphor, a poetic dimension beyond the endless medical measuring and the colloquial countdown to your 'arrival'. I am lichen, I have become a creature made of two distinct but co-dependent bodies. You cannot yet exist without me and without you I'll likely continue to exist but I'd no longer be me. But then, it has to move on, no one metaphor can carry all there is in the politics of pregnancy or the mysteries of becoming.[6]

The ecology of the ontogenetic body: mothering

Reeve's 'Ecological Body' foregrounds how the body is in continuous "flux, participation and change" (2011: 51). The movement with and through the changing environment of another body and the world beyond it creates a palpable awareness of the mutability and undetermined sense of self.

This is not to reduce the mother-body simply to a passive environment as the reduction of woman to landscape and vice versa has a long history in the service of domination of both. To focus on the rhythms, patterns and fluidity of development brings us in part to the mother-body. However, as the ontogenetic body is relational it points to the necessity of opening up the experience of pregnancy beyond the already overburdened mother by acknowledging and remembering that every body has experienced pregnancy, that is, *every body* has come from *some body* no matter how they are parented thereafter. Each experience is unique and tells its own story through its own improvisatory dance. That dance has a basic movement and structural vocabulary; one that informs how we move through our lives. Through BMC and related practices we can re-calibrate our awareness and re-direct our attention as necessary. So while the ontogenetic body has an immediate application for those working with infants, in fact the patterns take us right through our lives, structuring our movement as an alphabet does a language.[7]

---

6   Paul Whelan (2011) recounts two very different metaphoric descriptions used to convey the dual nature of lichens in the late 1800s when they were variously described as a master-slave or tyrant-captive damsel dyads. See also Iris Marion Young's essay 'Pregnant Embodiment: Subjectivity and Alienation' for a further detailed discussion of the paradox of subjectivity in pregnancy where she argues that pregnancy "reveals a paradigm of bodily experience in which the transparent unity of self dissolves and the body attends positively to itself at the same time that it enacts its projects" (2005: 47).

7   Bainbridge Cohen (2008: 122-156). Here she discusses and describes the 'The Alphabet of Movement: Primitive Reflexes, Righting Reactions and Equilibrium Responses'.

The ontogenetic body is a way of moving and a mode of perception. It makes us aware of developmental processes and gives us a method for embodying the forms, mind states and movement patterns of our cellular histories. This can challenge the ways in which we see every body and opens our eyes to our interconnections and inter-vulnerabilities. It is beyond the scope of this chapter to address the complex and often fraught issues of motherhood but it brings a focus to the ontogenetic patterns at our disposal and reminds us of the mothering and parenting involved. By embodying our earliest pathways we have a chance to (re)-parent ourselves, to re-pattern our choices, to find new ways to perceive and move in and with our worlds.[8]

Pre-vertebrate and vertebrate patterns

BMC founder, Bonnie Bainbridge Cohen summarises the ontogenetic and BASIC NEUROLOGICAL PATTERNS she mapped through BMC as follows:

> "The developmental material includes primitive reflexes, righting reactions, equilibrium responses and the Basic Neurological Patterns. These are the automatic movement responses that underlie our volitional movement. The reflexes, righting reactions and equilibrium responses are the fundamental elements, or the alphabet, of our movement. They combine to build the Basic Neurological Patterns (BNP), which are based upon pre-vertebrate and vertebrate movement patterns."[9]

In a training or exploration session the patterns can be separated out, investigated individually, played with openly, and brought to consciousness. However, at maturity, all the patterns are present at once in some way, even if it is as a marked absence. It is important to note also that BMC is always concerned with the whole person and the full range of embodied experience, so that if patterns or reflexes or systems are singled out they are then ultimately re-integrated into the whole person. The BNPs are both movements and structures; the patterns are a moving support structure – we carry it with us and are carried by it; to live is to continually embody such paradoxes.

---

8   The ontogenetic body in this way highlights the restrictions and limitations of access to material choices that many bodies encounter and, in particular, access to reproductive choices for women in Ireland today.

9   Bainbridge Cohen (2008: 5) and Glossary.

While we can identify and embody these patterns and find the support they offer, there are still many unanswerable questions: what makes patterns? What are the invisible forces at play? That is, what is the unique combination of gravity and desire that acts on each body, that provokes these ancient and on-going patterns? What environments, internal and external, can support and provoke the full expression of anyone's particular articulation of this shared physical vocabulary?

Watery world

I go to the pool. You hang, you dangle, you skip within me. We go under. I let my spine dissolve and enter into your fluid world. We breathe together; I follow your lead; I let go. My whole body breathes as one entity... I am floated by the water, moved by the wake. Together we wait, I feel you pulse, and I follow, rolling and extending. We glide in a game of stop and go, of hide and seek, that we'll be playing for a long good time together I hope.

Bainbridge Cohen explains: "Development is not a linear process but occurs in overlapping waves with each stage containing elements of all the others. Because each previous stage underlies and supports each successive stage, any skipping, interrupting, or failing to complete a stage of development can lead to alignment/movement problems, imbalances within the body systems, and problems in perception, sequencing, organisation, memory, and creativity" Bainbridge Cohen (2008: 4). Exploring one's own embodiment of the patterns can bring new awareness to our moving structures, to what aspects feel easeful or where there may be gaps in the sequence.

For performers, the ontogenetic patterns offer a means of analysing their own movement habits and also provide a playful framework for characterisation or movement vocabularies. In BMC, embodying a pattern or a body system is described as also having a particular quality of 'mind'. In performance this quality can support a specific expressive need whether in the discovery of new choreographies, character choices, support for vocal expression or of atmospheric co-presence.

19

Conclusions for now

What we carry and what we let go

You have been carried. And you carry and are carried by all that patterns you.

Carry on.

My son is now two years old. Today he says, 'no kiss' when I leave for work. He is a busy toddler with his own full agenda. Only when he's sick or tired do I get the luxury of closeness we shared in the earliest part of his life. When he comes back to me for that comfort he likes playing with my belly button. Sometimes this isn't very comfortable, but I like him connecting to my centre through the point where I connected to my mother. He plucks at the imaginary ancestral line to play his own notes reminding me of the necessity and fragility of those connections, as well as the way they become internalised and seem to disappear. I chide myself that this is overly romanticising something simple. Then he tells me my belly button has a moon in it, and so I give in to its gravitational pull.

Performance practices and somatic playfulness offer us avenues to explore the ontogenetic body and in turn that body supports performance and opens up the potentiality of creative impulses. This body is just one of many possible approaches in the rich terrain of Body-Mind Centering which explores all body systems in depth as well as developmental movement patterns. Everybody, that is every body, has journeyed along their originary pathways of the ontogenetic body in their own particular way. While we can name certain developmental milestones it is not a straightforward trail with a predestined arrival point. There are culs de sac, switchbacks and setbacks, leaps forward, interesting by-passes, scenic highlights, which all the while sustain us in the daily plodding along. Performance reminds of this perpetual motion of subjectivity as well as the desire for its stabilisation. If we follow Ericka Fischer-Lichte's definition of performance as that which requires 'bodily co-presence', then the ontogenetic body shows us that this is an inherent condition of our existence and that performative playfulness is at the core of being.

Dr. Róisín O'Gorman is a theatre artist and lecturer at University College Cork, Ireland. She studied theatre in the USA and returned to Ireland in 2007. Róisín's current research lives between embodied practices and theoretical understandings of performance. She explores this interdisciplinary terrain through the somatic practice of Body-Mind Centering (BMC) which offers an embodied ground to her theoretical and media-based work. Róisín completed her Somatic Movement Educator certification in BMC with Embody-Move Association in the UK with support from UCC and The Arts Council of Ireland.

r.ogorman@ucc.ie

Acknowledgements

Many thanks to workshop participants and collaborators who have played with me in exploring the ontogenetic body and risked new territories of experience. Also thank you to Sandra Reeve for her engagement throughout this process and to Emma Meehan and Natalie Garrett for their careful reading of earlier versions of this work.

Bibliography

Bainbridge Cohen, B. (2008) 2nd ed. *Sensing, Feeling, and Action: The Experiential Anatomy of Body-Mind Centering,* Northampton, MA: Contact Editions

Fischer-Lichte, E. (2008) *The Transformative Power of Performance,* (trans. Jain, S.), London and New York: Routledge

Hartley, L. (1995) *Wisdom of the Moving Body,* Berkeley, CA: North Atlantic Books

Reeve, S. (2011) *Nine Ways of Seeing a Body,* Axminster: Triarchy Press

Whelan, P. (2011) *The Lichens of Ireland,* Cork: The Collins Press

Wright Miller, G. *et al.* (2011) *Exploring Body-Mind Centering: An Anthology of Experience and Method,* Berkeley, CA: North Atlantic Books

Young, I.M. (2005) *On Female Body Experience: 'Throwing like a girl' and other essays,* Oxford: Oxford University Press

The Inter-subjective Body

Natalie Garrett Brown

Abstract

This chapter introduces the inter-subjective body as a further expression of the Ecological Body discussed in the first book in this series (Reeve, 2011). Notions of the body in flux and co-created in relationship with the environment, for example, can be seen as central to both. Specific to the inter-subjective body, however, is an interest in the inter-relationship between dancing bodies. This focus thus brings a particular interest in corporeal exchange and the related ethical and political significances of subjectivity as co-created.

Theoretically this lens is informed by Deleuze and CORPOREAL FEMINISM and advocates an affinity between Deleuzian-inflected corporeal feminism and SOMATIC-informed movement practice. Both, it is suggested, offer a critique of the mind/body dualism implicit within humanist understandings of subjectivity. Accordingly each can be argued to re-cast subjectivity as an always-embodied activity, an inter-corporeal exchange between 'self', recast as shifting and multiple, and 'otherness'.

From this conceptual ground, the chapter proposes three key characteristics of the inter-subjective body within contemporary dance practice: the cultivation of a somatic mode of attention; touch as a mode of communication; and the possibility of corporeal exchange between dancers within the context of site-responsive performance practice.

Case studies drawn from the author's experience as a dance artist working in the field of somatic informed dance, accompany the discussion, and are offered to illuminate the formulation of the inter-subjective body.

(2001) Alongside others, in a movement workshop drawing on BODY-MIND CENTERING (BMC), I'm asked to bring attention to the quality of elasticity and plasticity in the connective tissue within my body. As I move, the earlier hands-on work with my partner exploring this body system resonates with, and supports, my exploration. Individually and collectively we take time to sense and move from this place.

As we continue this inner exploration, a second invitation is offered and I/we are reminded of the external environment. As I continue to move I hear the suggestion that I might find relationship with the walls or the floor of the studio as a way of increasing awareness of the spine; I try this. Partially succeeding, I am helped by the reminder that the body might connect with ground or surface through yielding and pushing – movement development patterns I have come to know in previous explorations. I continue with this possibility and notice myself experiencing a dynamic suspension in my moving self as I shift my attention between inner connective tissue and the outer space of dance studio.

Improvising with these somatic images, sourced experientially, I am reminded of the inter-connection between the spaces of the body and the 'real' space(s) outside the body.

The inter-subjective body might be understood as a further expression of the 'ecological body' outlined in the first volume in this series, in that it resonates with notions of the body as co-created in relationship with the environment and thus not characterised by stasis. It is a lens which revisions humanist understanding of self as stable and given, thereby aligning with contemporary philosophical concerns that presuppose an interconnection of mind and body.[1] Specific, however, to the inter-subjective lens is an interest in the inter-relatedness of bodies, considered here through an exploration of corporeal exchange between dancers.[2]

The case studies offered in this chapter are drawn from my experiences as a dance artist over the last ten years.[3] In particular my work as a dance artist is coloured by an advocacy of the interconnectedness of theory and practice, and interest in somatic practices, specifically Body-Mind

1   See Reeve (2011) for a succinct account of post-humanist understandings of subjectivity.

2   As Stephanie Skura (1990: 183) observes, the somatic dancing subject argued for here is dissimilar from that found in conventional modes of dance-making which privilege the visual, placing the choreographer as outside 'eye/I', arranging objectified bodies in space and time. A focus on detailed and accurate replication of complex movement sequences and spatial patterns derived by the single choreographer from a visual perspective can be seen to shore up aspects of humanist subjectivity through its privileging of the 'logic of visualisation'. I argue that somatic-informed dance can disrupt this ocularcentrism through a process of creating and performing which emphasises the continued exploration of movement responses to the experientially sourced image or score through the kinaesthetic and the visual realm, not just the latter.

3   The framing of these case studies as examples of the inter-subjective body began in my doctorate studies (Brown, 2007).

Centering (BMC).[4] This interest has informed a collaborative, site-responsive project called *enter & inhabit*. Begun in 2007, *enter & inhabit* explores process-driven dance-making in public sites characterised by flow and transition. The project includes durational movement improvisation, photography and writing to create live and virtual installations and is drawn upon in the case studies included here.

This chapter, therefore, offers a play between the hypothetical and the real case study. The reflections offered here, while grounded in my experience, are multi-stranded in their references and untethered in linear time and space. They are further characterised by the range of subject positions from which they are written. At times I am the observer, at others the observed. Within this approach the case study examples seek to offer accumulating perspectives on key experiences that for others and myself point towards a manifestation of the inter-subjective body in western contemporary dance practice.[5] Thus, in the following pages, overlapping layers of the inter-subjective body are unveiled through an interplay between case study and theoretical reflections, inviting the reader to think and feel into this lens as a lived possibility. In offering this lens, I propose three key characteristics of the inter-subjective body within contemporary dance practice:

- the cultivation of a somatic mode of attention
- touch as a mode of communication
- the possibility of corporeal exchange between dancers within the context of site-responsive performance practice.

The inter-subjective lens rests upon a presupposition of the inter-connection of mind and body and, in so doing, undermines the idea of the body as a sealed, predetermined and given entity and instead suggests the boundaries of the body as permeable – allowing embodied experience, a dialogue between inner and outer, self and other to constitute subjectivity understood as an emergent and ongoing process. This is something argued

---

4   For BMC and somatics, see the glossary. For more on BMC see Cohen (1993) or Hartley (1989).

5   Here I am drawing on a theorisation of this term as offered by dance scholars informed by corporeal feminism. However this term is used by others working in the fields of psychoanalysis, psychology and philosophy, specifically phenomenology, when formulating understandings of relationship.

for by corporeal feminists informed by the philosophy of Deleuze and explores the notion of multiple subjectivities created via the mind/body's continuous interrelation with dynamic structures of power as an alternative to the humanist notion of the stable subject.[6]

Cultivating a somatic mode of attention; subjectivity as inherently embodied

Alongside two other workshop participants I am led through a hands-on exploration to invoke awareness of the cerebrospinal fluid [7] (CSF), the fluid that bathes the brain and flows up and down the spinal column. We take turns in the shifting roles. One lying down to receive the hands-on work while two others use a 'light', 'listening' touch to offer sensorial feedback, placing hands-on over the three areas where, for BMC, the pulse of the CSF is palpable: base of the skull, tail bone and ankles.

In this exploration I came to know experientially an aspect of the body, my body, that I had only previously grasped intellectually through the theorising of anatomy images on the page. As I offer hands-on it takes me time to perceive the flow of CSF in my partner's body but eventually I became aware of the slow pulsating rhythm of the fluid, slower than the rhythm of the breath and characterised by a wave-like, rippling flow of sensation from the ankle up to the skull.

When receiving this touch, however, I am surprised by how different my experience is in contrast to when I was listening to another's. Rather than having a specific sense of the flow of the fluid I had just experienced, I am left with a sense of being settled, deep in the body, my usual availability to language momentarily absent and my limbs and torso experienced as one integrated entity.

---

6   I discuss this point further in Brown (2011).

7   BMC brings attention to the high proportion of fluids that form the material body, thereby challenging muscle and bone as the major substances of the body. The Fluid System is seen to consist of cellular, intercellular, blood, lymph, cerebrospinal (CSF) and synovial fluids: all distinguishable but fully interrelated in terms of their function and physical properties. Fluids are understood to move through the different systems of the body, merging, transforming, and intersecting as they fulfil their function within the whole. Cohen, the originator of BMC, says, "All the fluids are essentially one fluid – largely made up of water – that changes properties and characteristics as it passes through different membranes, flows through different channels and interacts with different substances" (Cohen, 1994: 67).

This possibility of attentive listening to another through the CSF with this doubling sensation of inner and outer, self and other comes with me as the group moves into a Contact Improvisation score. Beginning solo, we play with the possibility of allowing our own movement to emanate from attention to the CSF, before opening up our awareness to the others moving in the space and finally allowing a transition into selective response to others.

As we reflect back on the experience of dancing the given score, one participant, experienced in the form of Contact Improvisation, comments that remaining with his attention on the CSF had enabled him to shift effortlessly in and out of new and changing partnerships throughout the improvisation – a comment echoing my own experience.

Reflecting on the experiences of others in this workshop and remembering my own journey through the CSF improvisation, particularly the sense of availability and receptivity I experienced when dancing with others, I am reminded of Albright's observation that some contemporary dance practices can be understood to cultivate a dual attention to inner and outer sensation. This involves a balancing of receptivity, perception and response which in turn enables dancers to experience and embody another's external or internal rhythm, shift in direction, movement or energy from moment to moment. Within this honed, somatic mode of attention, Albright suggests, is to be found a process which opens up the possibility that identity can be multiple and shifting, claiming that "in the midst of these improvisational exchanges of attention, gesture, sweat and energy one is trained to confront an other in such a way as to confound the usual distinctions between self and 'other'"(Albright, 2001: 1).

Developing this further, Albright suggests that contemporary dance practices that cultivate a somatic mode of attention can serve to shift a dancer's embodied knowledge of his/her relationship with the world. "By shifting our somatic imagination, we can reorder our cultural notions of selfhood... the self becomes an interdependent part which flows through and with the world" (*ibid*: 3). In so doing, the humanistic assumption that the creation of self is distinct from, and unrelated to, corporeal other is brought into question and the embodied and emergent quality of subjectivity is once more realised.

"If the world is already inside one's body, then the separation between self and other is much less distinct. The skin is no longer the boundary between the world and myself, but rather the sensing organ that brings the world into my awareness. In this intersubjective space in which one can be penetrated by sensations both external and internal, the heretofore unquestioned separation of individual and the world (or me and you) becomes more fluid. What I am talking about here is the possibility of re-conceptualizing the physical borders of bodies through attention to sensation." (Albright, 2003: 262)

As such, her work can be understood to evoke the possibility that moving with and from a somatic mode of attention serves to create an inter-subjective space, a shared third space in which a series of momentary meetings and interrelations between self and 'other', conceptualised as individual or environment, offers subtle shifts and changes in the individual's first person perspective [from the soma] of self, thereby experientially demonstrating subjectivity to be a process of becoming; one that is non-monolithic and wholly embodied.

Albright's assertion that certain forms of contemporary dance can create an 'inter-subjective space' foregrounds the need to move on from a position of identity politics. In doing so, she acknowledges the importance of the essentialist/constructivist feminist debate in unveiling how Western philosophy rests upon a division of the world into oppositional categories, mind/body, self/other and the extent to which these were offered as the 'natural' order of things. She therefore recognises the ways in which feminism has disrupted the hierarchies this had held in place and proposes that it is necessary to re-conceptualise difference as 'always in motion' (Albright, 2001: 2).

Using the imagery of a dance form familiar to herself, Contact Improvisation, she argues that in order to step outside the binaries of Western philosophical structures of thought, we must 'launch ourselves across that metaphysical slash between self/other' (*ibid:* 2). Such claims as to the significance of dance forms, which foreground motility in understandings of difference, might also be made about site-responsive projects and outdoor-dance practices. For example within the *enter &* *inhabit* project there is a desire to work in spaces and places characterised by flow and transition. These have variously included ring roads, river crossings, plazas, common pathways and symposium corridors and give us a heightened experience of the inherent change to be found in all environments. Sometimes we have moved in the same sites repeatedly through the seasons, a process which once more re-inscribes the quality of change to be experienced in these places and spaces as ever-present and emerging.

This we might understand as a Deleuzian becoming, whereby the tension between original and copy becomes obsolete and a flat hierarchy of difference pervades. Or to explore this another way, as we move in these sites of change, witnessing our own activity of sensing, perceiving and response, we are simultaneously attuned to the shifts and stillness present in our constellation of three, and the emerging space and place we co-create. And in this constellation of three, we develop and hone, moment to moment, our doubling of attention to soma and other, co-creating a third or inter-subjective space which emanates not from a merging or collapse of one into the other but rather derives from the vitality of both in attentive conversation, a multi-directional listening through the body.

Touch as a mode of communication; subjectivity as co-created and relational to other

(2001/2002) Seated in a circle, amongst a group of experienced dance artists during a workshop exploring BMC I listen to a discussion on the sense of touch, touch as continuum of possibilities, a dialogue between receiver and giver. At one end of this sliding scale the receiver is considered an active recipient. The giver of touch is there primarily to support and offer a 'sounding board' for his/ her partner's experience. At the opposite end the giver takes some body weight and strongly guiding or directing the movement of the receiver's body, whether that is internal or external. In between these two extremes exists the possibility that the giver 'listens' via touch to his/her partner, and connects with his/her flow of energy in order to follow and stay with it and to emphasise and direct the receiver's existing movement, or gently but consciously suggest another option or direction.

We move to a partner to explore this continuum and the felt sense of this possibility. I realise a few years on that this informs my own practice working in the outdoors. Writing reflectively on an experience of a duet improvisation from an interest in surface and sensation I note how the sense of touch and an opening of all the senses, not just the visual, underlies my continuing exploration of an inter-subjective being in the world through my own collaborative creative practice...

As we have seen in this lens, subjectivity arises through our being in the world and central to this is an acknowledgement of the role of touch and movement in relating, communicating and comprehending space. While the ocularcentric nature of western culture privileges the I/eye in conceptualisations of self, contemporary dance practices that cultivate a somatic mode of attention implicitly question this hierarchy of the senses. In deconstructing this hierarchy of the senses, subjectivity is revealed as a process of becoming through the sensory-perceptual feedback loop that relies on all the senses, not just the ocular.

For example, in sympathy with the philosophy of Merleau-Ponty, BMC recognises that one can touch and be touched in many different ways. Underlying this is an understanding that in touching, the individual is simultaneously touched, a constant inter-corporeal process that invokes a cycle of responses via the regulating neurological feedback systems of the body. This acknowledgement of the tactile exchange of information between self and other is conceived of as always present, a continuum of potential rather than something that is either present or absent. This understanding of touch is advocated too by Deane Juhan, who writes:

> "We can never touch just one thing; we always touch two at the same instant, an object and ourselves, and it is in the simultaneous interplay between these two contiguities that the internal sense of self – different from both the collection of body parts and the collections of external objects – is encountered... my tactile surface is not only the interface between my body and the world, it is the interface between my thought processes and my physical existence as well. By rubbing up against the world I define myself to myself." (Juhan, 1987: 34)

The idea of touch as inherently inter-subjective is substantiated by a number of evolutionary and biological 'truths' offered by scientific enquiry. In particular, Juhan draws attention to the development of touch in the embryo, cited to take place as early as week six. He also emphasises the shared origin of the nervous system and skin tissue, both of which are seen to develop from the ectoderm layer of the early embryonic cells.

Maintaining a simultaneous awareness of inner and outer sensory information, dancers working with a somatic mode of attention and informed by practices such as BMC relate to each other in space through a corporeal exchange rather than recourse to the visual. The corporeal interrelationship between dancers has various manifestations depending on the artist's particular experience and interest. However, common to many of them is a conscious dismissal of sight as *the* way a dancer can be aware of another in space. In particular, their relationship is characterised by the use of touch, a felt sense or kinaesthetic awareness of each other and an increased attention to sound. And in this multi-sensory communication between dancers and place, the inter-subjective body, is evoked once more.

A case for flattening the hierarchy of the senses and recognising touch as inherently central to subjectivity is made similarly by Manning (2007) with reference to Tango as an improvisational form. That the hegemony of humanist subjectivity can be disrupted by a re-ordering of the senses, a de-privileging of the visual via a foregrounding of touch, is taken as a given by Manning. Making this point she prefaces her study by stating:

> "I explore the ways in which research on the senses can extend beyond commonsense approaches to the senses and to the body. To write about the senses it is necessary to write against the grain of a mind-body reason-senses model that continues to privilege staid readings of gender, biology, and politics." (Manning, 2007: xii).

Underlying this assertion lies the recognition that "the rational modern subject" is one incompatible with "a sensing body in movement" (*ibid*: 159) and as such her reading of Tango resonates with the major themes and concerns of the discussion here.

The particular understanding of touch that Manning offers is in sympathy with Juhan's identification of touch as inherently inter-subjective (described above). She notes for example, as Juhan does, the biological development of touch *in utero* and the significance of touch to the healthy development of young in both humans and other mammals. Echoing BMC, she also highlights the way in which touch is an always-present sense and the skin the largest sense organ of the body. She thus re-casts the relationship between the senses and the body. In particular she takes issue with the model of one body giving or withholding touch from another to argue for the notion of "a stable body that exists in a pre-given space-time which contains an active giver and a passive receptor" (*ibid*: xiii). In contrast to this, Manning argues for "positioning the senses *relationally* as expressions of moving bodies" (*ibid*) which thus leads to:

> "...not a subjective body that identifies itself as something concrete one could call a *self* or an *individual*, but a series of intensities, through which endlessly diverse populations are engendered."
> (*ibid*: 95)

Corporeal exchange and dancing inter-subjectivity

(2011) Moving in relation to my collaborator, aware of the sound of her moving, a shared interest in perching, shifting, a play of form and constellation emerges. Amongst this my own interests momentarily fall to the fore before merging, and converging interests reassert themselves once more. In this I notice a shifting back and forth across the shared and the singular. Monitoring moments of fusion, alertness, quickening, whispers of slide and shimmer against the surface of the earth appear followed by pause, stillness, rest. In the amphitheatre of sound I hear rich and full the depth of space mapped through bird call, trains, dogs, children's voices, and planes overhead. Slipping under, moving across I feel the appetite of my muscles to move, lean, find support and ground. We breathe and find shared stillness once more.

On another day I'm reminded once more, re-remembering as though stumbling upon a revelation, the subtle and detailed knowing of place and space that unfolds when moving with attention to skin and the sense of touch, in companionship with others also following the same score or task. Beginning with attention to my own and partner's breath as we sit in contact, I find my form as I meet the surface of the muddy, ivy strewn, leafy ground. In this a fluid spine, softened by the contact of my partner's breath guides my coming to know that place in that moment. Her materiality reminds me of mine. In tracing and tracking the detail of the ground I simultaneously experience the layered shifting fullness of my own being...

The sound of cars, ripple of stream, weave of branches and the mounding curving sweep of the bank edge lead me to a journey of reach and pull crawl along the mud, a mud which pours and creeps and I make the smallest of journeys through a cavern of time, from web to white mushroom before laying sideward to receive a droplet on the skin of my cheek moments before dislodged by my partner's moving, and clear but delicate sounding.

Manning suggests that recognising the inter-subjective quality of touch leads to a particular concept of space and time. This is different from that which emanates from the delineation of self and other – the humanist subject position. Importantly it is one whereby movement pre-exists space and time. Drawing on her example of Tango understood as an improvisational form, she highlights the way in which dance forms rooted in the sense of touch can function as a site for the expression of otherness within the dominant order, claiming:

> "Tango will remain the dance of the milieu – the in-between… It is
> not the dance of cities or countries, but the dance of the ghetto, of
> the space that cannot be accurately named or defined." (*ibid*: 17).

Doing so leads her to share Albright's contention that a meeting of other with a somatic mode of attention leads to an experience of emergent subjectivity. In the moment to moment of improvising with a partner, claims Manning, each dancer is not reaching out towards a known, predetermined other or destination but rather moving forwards towards the not-yet-modulated or formed.

> "The body is the intermediary through which I create, with you,
> the shared space of our touch, our subjectivity-in-process. …Touch
> is a movement toward an other through which I recognize myself
> differently, spacing time as I time space." (*ibid*: 60)

Thus, for Manning, the inter-subjective body might be said to challenge the body politic of state sovereignty which rests upon a delineation between self and other. State politics, argues Manning, requires a stable body – one that is accountable as legitimate and appropriate as well as responsible within the organising principles and practices of the dominant order. Bodies of difference might claim to threaten and undermine this, their material excess a reminder of an embodied resistance to the body contained by boundaries.

"In a model of consensual politics, the citizen cannot have an unstable body, for that body would challenge the organization of the body-politic...The body, every body, and most certainly the 'nonexistent' body at the borders of the state, threatens the state's strict dichotomy between inside and outside. These deviant bodies emphasise the porosity of their mobile, sensing fleshiness." (*ibid*: 70)

(2012) We didn't apply to be there/here. In developing our outdoor practice over the last two years, we befriended the dogs and their human companions as they passed. We offered the visiting policeman our website address to validate our activity as art. In that moment one of us had an art for PR. He was responding to a call of concern. A concern for adult female bodies, sometimes in contact, paused or moving horizontal on the ground while a man with machine photographed close by. The word pornography was jokingly used. We were wearing rain gear and walking boots.

Dr. Natalie Garrett Brown, is principal lecturer in dance at Coventry University, UK, where she contributes to the BA (Hons) Dance course and co-ordinates postgraduate provision for the Performing Arts Department. She is associate editor for the *Journal of Dance and Somatic Practices* and sits on the editorial board for the Dancelines section in *Research in Dance Education*. Natalie has recently completed her Somatic Movement Educators Training in Body-Mind Centering with Embody Move Association, UK and is co-convenor of the International Conference for Dance and Somatic Practices, held biannually at Coventry University. Alongside this she is a founding member of *enter & inhabit*, a collaborative, site-responsive project and the Corporeal Knowing Network: an exchange between theatre and dance artists and scholars interested in embodied writing practices and process.
http://www.enterinhabit.com
http://c-dare.co.uk

Acknowledgements

I am indebted to an array of dance practitioners and scholars, in particular the teachings of Trisha Bauman, Katy Dymoke, Linda Hartley and Helen Poynor. Other voices, such as those of dance scholars Ann Cooper Albright and Erin Manning, are heard in the lines and pages of writing that dialogue with and between the case studies. Thanks also to Emma Meehan and Róisín O'Gorman for their insights and comments in the writing of this chapter.

Bibliography

Albright, A. C. (2001) 'Open Bodies: (X)changes of Identity in Capoeira and Contact Improvisation', Conference Proceedings, Congress on Research in Dance, *Cord 2001 Transmigratory Moves Dance in Global Circulation,* New York: New York University

Albright, A. and Gere, D. (2003) *Taken by Surprise, A Dance Improvisation Reader,* Middletown, CT: Wesleyan University Press

Banes, S. and Lepecki, A. (2007) *The Senses in Performance,* London: Routledge

Benedetto, S. (2007) 'Guiding somatic responses within performative structures' in Banes and Lepecki (2007)

Braidotti, R. (1991) *Patterns of Dissonance,* Cambridge: Polity Press

_____ (1992) 'On the female Feminist subject, or: from 'she-self' to 'she-other'' in Bock, G. and James, S. (eds.) *Beyond Equality and Difference,* London: Routledge

_____ (1994) *Nomadic Subjects, Embodiment and Sexual Difference in Contemporary Feminist Theory,* New York: Columbia University Press

_____ (2002) *Metamorphoses, Towards a Materialist Theory of Becoming,* Cambridge: Polity Press

Brown, N. G. (2007) 'Shifting ontology: somatics and the dancing subject, challenging the ocular within conceptions of western contemporary dance', PhD Thesis, Roehampton University, University of Surrey. [Unpublished]

_____ (2011) 'Disorientation and emergent subjectivity: The political potentiality of embodied encounter', *Journal of Dance and Somatic Practices* 3:1+2, pp.61-73

Carter, A. (1999) 'Dying Swans or Sitting Ducks? A Critical Reflection on Feminist Gazes at Ballet', *Performance Research* 4(3), pp.91-98

Cohen, B. B. (1994) *Sensing, Feeling, and Action; The Experiential Anatomy of Body-Mind Centering,* Northampton, MA: Contact Editions

Cohen, J. and Weiss, G. (2003) *Thinking the Limits of the Body,* New York: State University of New York Press

Deleuze, G. (1968/1994) *Difference and Repetition,* (trans. Pattern, P.), London: Athlone

Deleuze, G. and Guattari, F. (1972/1983) *Anti-Oedipus: Capitalism and Schizophrenia,* (trans. Hurley, R., Seem, M. and Lane, H.R.), Minneapolis, MN: University of Minnesota Press

_____ (1980/1987) *A Thousand Plateaus: Capitalism and Schizophrenia,* (trans. Massumi, B.), Minneapolis, MN: University of Minnesota Press

Dempster, E. (2004) 'Identities in Motion', *Dance, Identity and Integration,* International Dance Conference Proceedings, Taiwan, pp.104-111

Grosz, E. (1994) 'Sexual Difference and the Problem of Essentialism' in Schor and Weed, *The Essential Difference,* Indianapolis, IN: Indiana University Press

_____ (1994b) *Volatile Bodies, Toward A Corporeal Feminism,* Indianapolis, IN: Indiana University Press

_____ (1995) *Space, Time, and Perversion*, London: Routledge

_____ (2003) 'Histories of the Present and Future: Feminism, Power, Bodies' in Weiss, G. and Cohen, J. (eds.) *Thinking the Limits of the Body*, New York: State University of New York Press

Hanna, T. (1995) 'What is Somatics?' in Johnson, D. H. (ed.) *Bone, Breath and Gesture: Practices of Embodiment,* Berkeley, CA: North Atlantic Books

Hartley, L. (1983) 'Body-Mind Centering; An Introduction', *New Dance*, No. 27, Winter 1983

Holledge, J. and Tompkins, J. (2000) *Women's Intercultural Performance*, London: Routledge

Howes, D. (1991) *The Varieties of Sensory Experience: a Sourcebook in the Anthropology of the Senses*, Toronto: University of Toronto Press

Juhan, D. (1987) *Job's Body*, New York: Station Hill Press

Jay, M. (1999) 'Returning the Gaze: The American Response to the French Critique of Ocularcentrism' in Weiss, G. and Faber, H. F. (eds.) *Perspective on Embodiment: The Intersections of Nature and Culture,* London: Routledge

Johnson, D. H. (ed.) (1995) *Bone, Breath and Gesture: Practices of Embodiment,* Berkeley, CA: North Atlantic Books

Manning, S. (1997) 'The Female Dancer and the Male Gaze: Feminist Critiques of Early Modern Dance' in Desmond, J. (ed.) *Meaning in Motion: New Cultural Studies of Dance*, Durham, NC: Duke University Press

Manning, E. (2007) *Politics of Touch, Sense, Movement and Sovereignty*, Minneapolis, MN: University of Minnesota Press

Merleau-Ponty, M. (1945/2002) *The Phenomenology of Perception*, (trans. Smith, C.), London: Routledge

Miller, W. G., Ethridge, P. and Morgan, T. K. (2011) *Exploring Body-Mind Centering*, Berkeley, CA: North Atlantic Books

Olsen, A. (2002) *Body and Earth: An Experiential Guide*, Hanover, NH: University Press of New England

Reeve, S. (2011) *Nine Ways of Seeing A Body,* Axminster: Triarchy Press

Schusterman, R. (1999) 'Somaesthetics: a disciplinary proposal', *Journal of Aesthetics and Art Criticism*, 57 (3) pp.29-33

Skura, S. (1990) 'The Politics of Method' in *Reimaging America: The Arts of Social Change*, Philadelphia, PA: New Society Publishers, pp.183-189

Weiss, G. (1999) *Body Images: Embodiment as Intercorporeality*, London: Routledge

The Autobiographical Body

Somatic Practice and Object Relations

Emma Meehan

Abstract

Autobiography can be described as a personal narrative, but this chapter reveals how the 'personal' is highly dependent on the changing context. Outlining various forms of autobiographical performance, the chapter then focuses primarily on SOMATIC performance practices that explore autobiography as a fluid experience based on relationships with other people and places. Drawing on OBJECT RELATIONS theory, which examines the relationship between subjective perceptions and external events, the author teases out ideas on the autobiographical body in performance training and production. Descriptions from training and performances provide examples of how autobiography is negotiated between mover and environment, along with indicating how such material can be developed for performance.

A number of objects are visible at the edge of the performance space – a teddy bear, some animal bones, a large cardboard box, a loaf of sliced white bread. A dancer chooses the cardboard box and pulls it into the centre of the space. The empty box lies on its side and the dancer dives into the open end of it, while her head bursts out the opposite side. Her arms and torso are tightly contained inside the box and she cries, "I'm not coming out!"

As I watch, I invent fleeting meanings for the scenario: a child having a tantrum, or an adult who is stuck and will not think 'outside of the box'.

A singer begins to make cooing, baby-like sounds, and then I start to imagine the dancer as a baby in the womb. A male mover enters the space and pulls on the flaps at the open end of the box, dragging its resistant weight with both hands. The box lifts slightly off the ground as he tugs it, while the song begins to sound like a baby crying. The combination of vigorous pulling and baby sounds do not disturb me, however, and I find myself laughing at the stubbornness of the dancer in the box.

As the male dancer tugs, the woman pushes her head deeper into the box, and curls her feet tightly into her chest, refusing to come out. The man continues to drag the box around the space and suddenly it rips open, revealing the female dancer's fragile frame curled up inside. I breathe a sigh of relief, relaxing as I imagine her body releasing out into the air from inside the confines of the box. But she yells, "No, no, no", as she pulls the box back over her body. The box falls open again and she says, "Oh damn it", as the audience laughs loudly.

I recall this piece from fragments of memory, lost somewhere between remembering and imagining. Layers are put together from the live performance, notebooks, film footage and impressions left behind by the event. The process of writing about the performance reveals new associations that appear in the re-performing of the piece both in my mind's eye and kinaesthetic memory.[1]

Now that I re-visit the performance, there is slight shock at the clarity with which I see a birthing narrative in the performance, which was only a vague notion at the time. What remains in my writing is a distillation of the piece, but also a reflection of my own interaction with the performance, filtered through personal lenses as a student with the choreographer of the work and as a researcher with a desire to make sense of these experiences.

This performance segment is part of a larger project called *Maya Lila* developed by Irish choreographer and movement therapist JOAN DAVIS.[2] Davis often performs outdoors and builds interactive environments to invite the audience into a multi-sensory experience of the dance. She has developed a form of improvised performance practice drawing from the somatic forms of AUTHENTIC MOVEMENT and BODY-MIND CENTERING. These movement forms reveal personal movement styles,

---

1   Kinaesthetic sense can be described as the perception of movement in space. See Kartsaki (2011).

2   Davis's books (2007a and 2007b) offer a detailed description of her methods and performances. In describing her work, I use the term 'improvised' to depict how the performance unfolds without pre-planning the content, although there is extensive somatic training and movement preparation for performances. (See glossary for further detail.)

patterns of behaviour and narratives that I suggest are autobiographical. Personal material often appears in her workshops or rehearsals, and Davis (2007a: 3) proposes that there is a connection between art and therapy in her practice. Her performances also emphasise the role of the audience as witness and co-creator in the way its members participate, inform and interpret the presented work and so I argue that the autobiographical material of the audience is also involved.

Writing from the perspective of audience-participant, I convey my perceptions based on subjective viewpoints from within the training and performances. In this sense, the autobiographical body of the title relates not only to the work that I describe, but also to the body of writing that is produced from my engagement with this performance practice. Too often it seems as though the body and written language are placed in binary opposition to each other. While they are comprised of different matter and texture, I believe that they are interrelated on a fundamental level, in how we frame and reflect on behaviours in everyday life. Examples of this range from being verbally encouraged to crawl and walk as children, to the physicality of the acts of speaking and writing. I knit embodied experience with written language in this chapter, and I invite readers to feel their bodies engaging as they read.

I suggest that autobiographical material derives from an ongoing, shifting set of relations, where individual autobiographies intersect with the wider environment to create collaborative autobiographies. While Davis's approach to somatic movement practice centres on the subjective experience and impulses of the mover, these come from being in relationship with people, places and events. In addition, the movement is informed by embodied personal histories from past relationships that impact behaviours and perceptions in the present time. Davis's work examines the 'intersubjective' space, described by Natalie Garrett Brown as the "interplay between an ever-emerging 'self' and 'otherness'" (2011: 70). As a mover in Authentic Movement practice,[3] I make contact with another body and feel shared sensations of heat and weight at the same

---

3   In Authentic Movement, the mover physically expresses movement impulses (often in a group of other movers) while a witness observes their own response to the movement. (See glossary for further detail.)

time becoming aware of the boundary of skin. I also come to realise how my body-mind responds to the meeting, with changes in pulse, sensation, breath, thought and feeling. This responsiveness extends out to include the relationship with the whole environment, as each context evokes different kinaesthetic reactions.

Of course, this is complicated by perceptions of 'body' and 'self' in different social and cultural contexts. The attachment to a sense of separate, individual identity or belonging to a collective identity can alter how a person frames their life e.g. by profession, nationality or personal qualities. Perhaps Davis's 'box piece' reflects a desire to stay neatly contained within a bounded and clear individual identity. Attachment to a collective identity has other issues, however, as seen in the brutality spurred by extreme nationalism. On either end of the spectrum, I see these as attitudes that do not acknowledge the somatic experience of exchange between individual and collective. I consider autobiography as a negotiated, relational and ongoing practice and suggest that this could inform the ways in which autobiography, a common trope in contemporary performance, can be explored and presented on stage.

Traditionally, the term autobiography has connotations of a linear, personal narrative. Celebrity autobiographies often chart significant life moments leading to personal success but these are usually written with the aid of ghost writers, managers, agents and PR personnel, framing personal life according to readers' perceived tastes and expectations. Such writing is shaped and packaged into a single story, often refuted by competing biographies that claim to tell the 'real' story behind an individual's climb to fame. The idea that an autobiography can fully represent someone's life or that life follows a clear, single path or even the idea of an 'individual' life are questionable, considering that, in this example, it is facilitated by processes of selection and collective writing. Another example of contemporary autobiographical narrative is the worldwide phenomenon of 'reality' television, which commodifies the personal narratives and 'real' characters that appear on the screen for mass consumption. In these examples, 'true-to-life' stories are formed in retrospect, piecing together moments that create a coherent storyline, rather than recognising the multiplicity of unfolding chance, choice, dead-ends and re-routing than occurs, or taking into account the impact of historical, social, cultural and political contexts on the direction of 'individual' lives.

Autobiographical performance today often highlights the problems with the idea of a linear and individualistic understanding of autobiography. Linda Park-Fuller (2000) and Joanne Gilbert (1997) list a wide array of contemporary autobiographical forms from rap music to Boal's Theatre of the Oppressed to stand-up comedy. This broad range of practices destabilises assumptions about what constitutes an autobiographical narrative, using methods such as group storyboarding, poetic representation, parody or mixing lived experience with imagined possibilities. Postmodern performance often deliberately obscures differences between fact and fiction in order to highlight how personal autobiographical narratives are constructed, as well as highlighting the autobiographical body of the performer as a site for reflecting what bodies represent and provoke.

As mentioned earlier, Davis practises somatic movement forms, an umbrella term for movement practices that emphasise body-mind integration, the agency of the subject in developing his/her own movement and the capacity for reflection in movement. Somatic forms usually bring attention to psycho-physical body histories, developing an awareness of restrictions to movement and expanding the range of movement to create a wider repertoire of responses. Thomas Hanna (1995), a physical therapist, applied the term 'somatic' to contemporary body-mind practices to illustrate his emphasis on the internal physical experience of the client as part of the process of improving movement capacity. Linda Hartley (2004: 11) links the idea of the self-sensing somatic body back to ancient practices such as yoga, meditation and shamanism, while Martha Eddy (2009: 6) notes that developments in the fields of dance, phenomenology and psychoanalysis have brought about the more recent validation of somatic practices in the West. The application of somatics in performance is an expanding field internationally, with the incorporation of diverse somatic forms into theatre and dance training as well as performance-making.

In a more traditional framework of the singular autobiography, the question could be asked: in Davis's 'box piece' described earlier, whose autobiographical story is it? Is it created by Davis who chooses the object, by the singer who creates the 'baby-like' sounds, by the male mover who drags the box around the space, or by the audience member who interprets what they see? Davis begins the story by following her impulse to dive into the box, but the narrative is also developed through her relationships with those surrounding her. This reflects somatic trainings where the behaviour patterns of the individual are understood as emerging from their interaction with the environment. Somatic-based performance can therefore serve as a useful case study to contribute to defining and analysing the autobiographical body. While my experience of somatic performances has helped me to understand autobiography as mutating and inter-relational, I also consider that this could inform the development of autobiography in performance more generally. I am interested in moving away from a strict sense of telling one's own story and towards understanding how the personal is informed by contexts prior to and during personal expressions in performance.

Returning to the intersection between my own autobiographical body and Davis's work, some of my experiences in training with Davis illustrate the somatic movement process. In Davis's workshops, the mover's first sensory experiences often focus on the contact between the floor and the body, and later with objects, as means of identifying patterns of relating. Below I describe a movement session with Davis that depicts how I make physical contact with the external environment in ways that reflect on my own life.

With my eyes closed, I reach into the space and find a tangled heap of soft wool with my hands. Drawing the material towards the centre of my body, I place the gentle texture against my stomach. I notice the full, expansive fleshiness of the wool in contact with my cold and tense body, curled in a ball on the floor. I imagine the woollen strands as spiralling, tangled intestines, spilling out onto the ground. I feel the springy strands of wool between my fingers and try to emulate the soft and pliable qualities of the wool, by rolling, breathing deeply, and stretching with pulsating movements. Absorbed in the experience, I become a twisting, turning, vibrant, messy, churning, expanding and contracting digestive system. I notice an emerging ease in my body as I play between feeling the texture of the wool and embodying my perception of the wool as guts, finding new possibilities for moving in the space.

In this sequence of movement, I became aware of my own habitual pattern of collapsing into the support of the floor, and I also found the 'guts' to try out new ways of softening and expanding my body. Contact with the floor and the wool as external objects became stimuli for investigating my relationship with self and space. By the end of the session, I noticed a sense of ease in my previously stiff body that came from playing with the texture of the wool, and embodying my perception of its qualities. A similar process of noticing movement habits can be used to understand how I make contact with other people. Through reflecting on responses when meeting other movers, the participant can start to note patterns of behaviour and explore new models of relationship as the work develops. An example of this can be drawn from a movement workshop where Davis invited the group to focus attention on the collective field.

With my eyes closed, I notice whistling and groaning sounds surrounding me, coming from some of the other workshop participants. Listening to the sounds, I imagine I am in a dark forest, with the wind blowing and trees creaking all around me. I move slowly through the space, feeling the weight of my hips and legs sinking with gravity and a deep heaviness pressing from my eyelids down to my toes. 'The weight of the world' occurs to me now as an expression for the burden I feel dragging me downwards. Reaching my hands out, I find another mover and hold on to her for support, tagging on to her shoulder as she progresses through the space. Now I feel more secure as I follow her buoyant body through what feels like the thick substance of the space.

Suddenly, I imagine that my feet are trapped under the roots of a tree. I can feel the sense of restriction to my feet that causes my breath to rise into my chest, as the image of a tangled web of gnarled roots comes to mind, in a kind of psycho-physical imagining. I know that, in fact, the body of another mover has rolled over my feet, but I am caught somewhere between the imagined and physical world. My grip on the first mover is slowly loosening as she continues to move onwards. My feet are trapped but my upper body strains forward as I hold on tightly to the advancing mover, for fear of losing the much-needed support. At the last moment, I am forced to let go of her arm, and feel a sense of release but also loss.

In this movement session, the collective field had an impact on my perceptions and imaginings, creating a fantasy world that came from my relationship with the sounds and touch of other movers. Contact with one mover's body allowed me to explore attachment and support, and later bumping into a different mover transformed my experience of the forest into a reflection on letting go. The entire autobiographical experience was informed by a co-created world, awakening imaginary, sensory and emotional reactions as well as altering my physical journey.

Like somatic practices, Object Relations theory also explores the idea of embodied autobiographies and interrelationships. Object Relations theory was developed in the 1940s in Britain by therapists such as W. R. D. Fairbairn, Melanie Klein and D.W. Winnicott. It focuses on the process of exchange between the individual and 'objects', referring particularly to other people. In Davis's teaching, she suggests that 'everything is object', as we have relationships not only with other people, but also with everything we encounter, such as parts of the body, places, things and so on. There is not sufficient space here to describe Object Relations practice in depth but I will introduce some aspects that are relevant to autobiography in performance. Davis brings attention to Object Relations in the performances, often demonstrated literally through the use of physical objects. A clear example of Object Relations can be seen at a performance where Davis moved with a bunch of pampas grass from her garden.

Davis sweeps the space with long green and white fronds of pampas grass, declaring that she is a cleaner who is a 'very obsessional worker'. She then brushes the feathery white fronds over the faces of audience members and three other dancers in the space. The dancers play together with the structure of their bodies, physical contact and spatial arrangements, while Davis finds nooks and crannies to clean. The contrast between Davis's focus on the action of dusting and the group of dancers involved in non-narrative, fluid movement provokes a dramatic tension.

Breaking this division, a dancer pulls a strand of the pampas grass from Davis's hands. Davis runs away, followed by the other dancers, creating a chasing game. Eventually, the group manage to entice Davis to link arms, creating a line of dancers rotating in a circular pattern in the space. After a number of rotations,

Davis breaks off and the 'cleaner' character disappears as she becomes absorbed in swinging the remaining pampas grass in figures of eight through the air.

In this piece, Davis projects 'dusting' qualities onto the object and then identifies with the role of cleaner. This intersects with ideas of 'projective identification' in Object Relations theory, described by Melanie Klein (1946: 147) as "the forceful entry into the object and control of the object by parts of the self". The child, and later the adult, projects aspects of the self onto an object, at the same time as maintaining a relationship with the object in order to control or make sense of it. In the 'cleaner piece', Davis is projecting qualities onto herself as well as the pampas grass. The body of an individual can then be both subject and object, as we can project onto ourselves and others, while they do the same. The audience's understanding of what they see can also be described as a form of projective identification, where qualities are projected onto the dancers as audience members try to make sense of what is happening in the space.

Projective identification is not presented as a fixed state in this scene. While engaged in this projective play, the impact of the other dancers on Davis's journey can be seen as her story eventually falls away, indicating the fluidity of collaborative narratives. Meanwhile, the other dancers appear to resist Davis's story, maintaining the integrity of their own movement which forms a counterpoint to hers. They do not merge or become the same in order to collaborate, but they are still interacting and negotiating the next steps of the unfolding choreography. The fronds of grass gently touch the faces of the dancers, perhaps awakening new sensations and impulses. They also try to relate to her by chasing and linking arms, so that her presence with them alters both their own activities and Davis's behaviour.

The audience in the piece also receive touch as they are brushed with the pampas grass. Davis's performances are usually highly interactive and sometimes audiences select objects to bring into the performance space or participate in games such as dressing up or taking on new names. Her installation spaces are designed to invite audience members to wander and play with instruments, boxes with surprise contents, threads for weaving, concave mirrors and so on. Collaboration can also take place by simply being in the space and witnessing the performance, responding on subtle levels through making eye contact, facial expressions, or shifting positions in space. In addition, Davis purposefully leaves gaps in performance narratives, to allow the audience's imagination to inform their interpretation of the work. For example, she does not offer a detailed plot in the 'cleaner piece' or 'box piece', but allows the audience to create the full story.

In *Autobiography and Performance,* Deirdre Heddon (2008: 8) postulates that the author and performer merge in autobiographical performance, but I would add to this that the 'auto' can also include the audience. My reading of Davis's 'box piece' at the time as a comic scenario is certainly informed by audience laughter as I participate in the group atmosphere. In retrospect, I am struck by the violence of dragging the box until it tears, and it appears to me now as a 'birthing narrative'. Of course, audience interpretation is inherent in any performance, but I suggest that creating a form of collaborative autobiography is also reliant on leaving space in the performance to involve people, the environment and surrounding circumstances as active factors.

However, a performance does not have to be improvised or completely interactive to allow the plurality of autobiography to be explored. In 2010, I created a performance called *Wellness Sensorium* based on the theme of hospital experience that was informed by my own personal background. However, I also wished to invite the audience to reflect on their own encounters with medical institutions. Drawing from Authentic Movement practice, I collected and re-worked a number of movement sequences, characters and scenarios related to the hospital theme with the help of two performers and three core mentors.[4] The sounds and smells of the hospital objects that I used as part of the rehearsal process often evoked visceral responses from me and my collaborators. For example, one wrote about the sound of the latex gloves reminding her of an uncomfortable gynaecological examination, while the smell of the sanitising spray gave me a queasy feeling in my stomach as I remembered time spent in hospital. I gathered written responses and hospital stories from friends and colleagues who participated in the process and work-in-progress showings. The 'final' piece was a solo performance, combining the collected material through projected

---

4   Performer-collaborators were Sue Mythen and Avril Tierney, and mentors included Margot Jones, Niamh Lawlor and Margaret Lonergan.

slides, voice-over, movement, object arrangements and story-telling, and was presented as part of an evening of body-based performance called *Transversal* in Dublin. During the evening, simultaneous performances were showing in different rooms of the venue and the audience could wander between spaces to capture snippets of each performance.

I stand in a large, grey concrete room, dressed in pyjamas, holding a bag with hospital objects – scrubs, stethoscope, doctor's notes, test tubes. A voice-over and projected titles tell me what action to take next. Titles such as 'boy with no balance', 'surgical hat', 'Dr. Power', 'desire to move, no energy to move' or 'kidney' are announced and I proceed by telling a story or performing actions that correspond to the slide. To my right, a cellist is warming up for a performance following mine. Behind me, a group of performance artists are constructing a set from found objects. Crowds of people enter from a door to the right. Some loiter, sit or stand and watch me. Others drift off and continue on to the next room through a door on the left.

The constant bustle brings me back to my memory of hospital – people coming and going, groups of students doctors and nurses looking, families visiting, new patients arriving, others going to surgery, and the restlessness of trying to sleep with the strange sounds around me. The voice-over calls out: "Parents leaving". In response, I recount a story I have collected from another person: "I am standing in a cot, watching my parents waving goodbye at the door before they leave me at hospital. I am two years old. In fact, it is my earliest memory." As I tell the story, I notice a man and woman standing in the left hand doorway of the room. I am surprised and wave to them from the hospital bed I have imagined in my mind's eye.

While I pre-rehearsed this piece, the audience movement around the building along with the sound of other performances added active elements which fed into the work. Sometimes surprising moments of coincidence occurred, creating resonances between the material and context. Sometimes contradictory juxtapositions brought about new responses from me that impacted the performance of the material. The option of wandering around the venue also offered audience members the opportunity to construct their own narratives from the glimpses they snatched at different times. It was also apparent, even though I was the primary creator and performer, that any performance is influenced by a wider group of supporting individuals that help in making and staging the work. To me, it was both informative and more representative of the process to include collective autobiographies, rather than focusing on creating an individualistic narrative.

In Object Relations theory, self-identity is constantly shaped in the play between self and other, and D.W. Winnicott (1971: 40-52) used the term 'transitional phenomena' to describe experiences that are both subject and object. For example, the 'transitional object' can be a toy or blanket that a child acquires and they experience it as both inside and outside the body, self and other simultaneously. Winnicott also describes the playing space between the mother and child as transitional, a 'potential space' to explore issues of connection and separation. He considers that transitional phenomena continue throughout life as a means of coming to terms with the relationship between self and other, along with suggesting that this playing turns into more developed creative forms. The idea of the potential space is conceptualised by Lisa Baraitser and Simon Bayly (2001: 65) as emulating the rehearsal process, where "the performance is not yet formed or fixed, identities remain fluid, performers can explore versions of themselves."

Somatic training methods offer a form of transitional space for trying out new behaviours and relationships, suspending the formation of set identities of 'self' and 'other'. The autobiographical body is also a transitional space, if we consider that autobiography is a provisional and evolving experience. This can be represented by embodying multiple, inter-personally negotiated autobiographies in the performance arena, like in Davis's role play as the cleaner or her character in the cardboard box. Here, she is both subject and object, projecting qualities of otherness onto the self and allowing external objects to stimulate subjective manifestations. In *Wellness Sensorium*, I also combined my own experiences of being in hospital with the stories, characters and movements of others, so I became a body in transition between selves and others. Even being in the performance space with a new audience awakened memories and reactions from me and hopefully sparked autobiographical stories for the viewer, suggesting that the performance arena is a transitional space of exchange.

As a lens for considering autobiographical and psycho-physical performance works, Object Relations theory demonstrates that the idea of 'personal' material is complex, considering the relational and illusory aspects of what can be considered autobiographical. That is not to say that we are merged with those around us, but we also cannot be defined as completely separate. Rather, I understand myself as 'in relationship' and try to bring awareness to boundaries, surfaces, contact, exchange and transitional spaces in between self and other as a way to know the autobiographical body. Through understanding the body not as an entirely separate entity but part of a system, I have come to appreciate the complexity of embodied autobiography in its constantly changing layers of personal experience and collective negotiation. This awareness can be brought to any performance that considers the autobiographical body as an emerging entity crossing between pasts, presents, audience, performer and environment.

Bryant Keith Alexander (2000: 102) proposes that once a personal narrative is shared, it can generate new autobiographies, so that "the autobiographical construct may serve as a road map designating a particular journey, but the generated autobiography may enter the journey at any point and chart its own meaningful course to self knowledge." As I watch Davis's performance of the 'box piece', I see her journey, but also interrupt the process with my own asides and interpretations, witnessing physical fact and projected fictions, suturing my own autobiographical history with the staged performance material. *Wellness Sensorium* also meshes my own perceptual engagement with the presence of other people and places, while I hope the audience can take the performance as a starting point for further journeys. My writing also comes from the space between the described performance works and my perceptions, past experiences and current reflections, creating an autobiographical story from the dialogue between self and other. The autobiographical body can then describe the 'body of work' that emerges as a performance unfolds and in the aftermath of the performance, allowing the prospect of reverberations and new directions not imagined within the performance itself.

Dr. Emma Meehan is a research assistant at Coventry University's Centre for Dance Research. She received her BA and PhD from the Drama Department, Trinity College Dublin, where she taught on the BA and MA programmes. She was also the administrator for the Arts Technology Research Lab at Trinity College. Funding and awards include: postgraduate studentships and awards from Trinity College, Artist in the Community Scheme Award and Travel and Training Award from the Arts Council of Ireland, Dance Ireland residencies and Sligo Arts Office Bursaries amongst others. Articles include: "Visuality, Discipline and Somatic Practices: The Maya Lila Performances of Joan Davis", in *The Journal of Dance and Somatic Practices*, Intellect Press, Vol. 2, No. 2, 2010, 219-232. She is a member of the Corporeal Knowing Network of researchers in the UK and Ireland exploring somatic practices in performance, and she is also on the board of Dance Research Forum Ireland.
meehanemma@yahoo.co.uk

Acknowledgements

I would like to acknowledge the support and feedback I received from Róisín O'Gorman and Natalie Garrett Brown in developing this chapter.

Bibliography

Alexander, B. K. (2000) 'Skin Flint (or, The Garbage Man's Kid): A Generative Autobiographical Performance Based on Tami Spry's Tattoo Stories', *Text and Performance Quarterly* 20, no.1, pp.97-114

Baraitser, L. and Bayly, S. (2001) 'Now and Then: Psychotherapy and the Rehearsal Process', in Campbell, P. and Kear, A. (eds.) *Psychoanalysis and Performance*, London: Routledge

Davis, J. (2007a) *Maya Lila: Bringing Authentic Movement into Performance – The Process.* Norfolk: Elmdon Books

——— (2007b) *Maya Lila: Bringing Authentic Movement into the World – The Offering.* Norfolk: Elmdon Books

Eddy, M. (2009) 'A Brief History of Somatic Practices and Dance: Historical Development of the Field of Somatic Education and its Relationship to Dance', *Journal of Dance and Somatic Practices* 1, no. 1, pp.5-27

Garrett Brown, N. (2011) 'Disorientation and the emergent subjectivity: The Political Potentiality of the Embodied Encounter', *Journal of Dance and Somatic Practices* 3:1+2, pp.61-73

Gilbert, J. (1997) 'Performing Marginality: Comedy, Identity, and Cultural Critique', *Text and Performance Quarterly* 17, no. 4, pp.317-330

Hanna, T. (1995) 'What is Somatics?' in Johnson, D. H. (ed.) *Bone, Breath, and Gesture: Practices of Embodiment*, Berkeley, CA: North Atlantic Books

Hartley, L. (2004) *Somatic Psychology: Body, Mind and Meaning*, London: Whurr

Heddon, D. (2008) *Autobiography and Performance*, Basingstoke: Palgrave Macmillan

Kartsaki, E. (2011) 'Writing and Re-writing: Performance Returns', *Activate* 1, no. 1, pp.1-9. http://www.thisisactivate.net/2011/05/14/writing-and-re-writing/

Klein, M. (1946/1996) 'Notes on Some Schizoid Mechanisms' in Scharff, D. E. (ed.) *Object Relations Theory and Practice*, Northvale, NJ: Jason Aronson Inc.

Park-Fuller, L. M. (2000) 'Performing Absence: The Staged Personal Narrative as Testimony', *Text and Performance Quarterly* 20, no. 1, pp.20-42

Winnicott, D.W. (1971) *Playing and Reality*, London: Routledge

The Resonant Body

Pam Woods

Abstract

The chapter identifies key moments in, reflects on, and provides insights into, the author's personal practice of 'Sounding Dance Improvisation' with specific focus on two case studies: movement and vocal performance investigations in response to different sites in Devon. It references some significant influences along the way, as it moves towards a definition of the Resonant Body in site-responsive improvisation. In considering what might be 'at play' in an 'unknowing' state, it calls to mind Guy Claxton's notion in *Hare Brain Tortoise Mind* (1997: 13) that slow ways of knowing "are receptive rather than proactive… and take seriously ideas that 'come out of the blue.'"

Introduction

A tiny disturbance within
Vibrations - expressed - Lady Louisa?
Resonance. Utterances.
Schism.
Me, space, Louisa, flashes of past, then in the present again.

The jottings above swiftly recorded an improvisation I performed in The Palm House at Bicton Gardens, Devon in 2002. Although some time ago, it marked an important stage in my postgraduate research, for which I adopted the term 'Sounding Dance Improvisation'.

'Resonance' was a word that was to arise many times in my process journal in different guises: resound; re-sound; sounding; sound inside; sound outside; sound again and again; vibrations; close connection; similarity in nature or character. Improvisation is widely accepted as a discipline of spontaneity and awareness, where "the content of the work is the content of the present" (Steinman, 1986: 78). For me the notion of 'resonance' also relates to the interplay between past and present. The layering of time within my practice relates to memory and also to the notion that performer and site may contain multiple 'histories'. This may be seen in the case studies presented here, along with some questions, observations and issues that have emerged for me during improvisatory performance projects as solo performer/creator working in response to 'site', also taken here to embrace 'place' and 'landscape'.

As Mike Pearson and Michael Shanks propose in *Theatre/Archaeology* (2001: 55):

> "Ecology may be defined as inhabitation – a broad and inclusive concept... Site, as concept, must be connected with place and locale, as the natural and cultural are entwined in a true ecology which moves beyond these familiar dualisms. So too we emphasise that site is as much a temporal as spatial concept – landscapes are enfolded; scenography works with the multidimensional temporality of memory, event and narrative."

'Choreography in the moment' perhaps aptly describes the solo 'Sounding Dance Improvisations' I perform. I choose non-arts sites, indoors and outside, of structural and acoustic interest, and work on the premise that sites *inform* the improvisations, the multifarious elements contained within them contributing to the overall choreography.

'Palm House' and 'Hermitage', Bicton Gardens, East Devon (2002)

The Palm House and the Hermitage were commissioned by Lord Rolle for his wife Louisa between 1820 and 1830. The former is constructed of 18,000 pieces of glass, the layout of the pathways and plant beds offering a range of spaces within a space. The latter is an unusual summer house overlooking a lake. I had established a relationship with the Palm House from previous visits[1] in 2001, so prior knowledge of the spaces and

---

1   I performed a series of improvisations over several weeks, on varying days of the week, at different times of day. The following provided sensory impulses and were part of the landscape informing them: the physical structure of The Palm House (metal arches, domed 'ceiling', wall, glass panes, decorative rosettes on metal girders); contents (pipes, ropes, trees, plants, paving stones, earth, iron grids, plant labels, smells and scents); outside (trees and plants, light and weather variables, fountain, wind, sounds of voices, people, birds, the garden's steam train); sounds produced as I improvised (tapping of my metal ring on metal pipes, my shoes on metal grid, vocal utterances).

acoustics informed my positioning for the first three improvisations in this case study:

1. by the door and pipes – corridor as far as a leafy palm as performance area
2. at the far end, at the corner where a significant curve of glass began
3. in the centre by the largest palm.

Palm House: Improvisation 1

Pipes hard, ropes, the knots, wall, decay, the smell too, leaf... then to the palm - a warmer place - soothing... the knots again... a little voice... bound, tense, a disturbance there? And then reaching to the wall up, up and then towards the palm again down, down to the label. The name of the palm - what was it? Playful now - a lighter moment - play on words, touch of humour, impish mood, laughter. Filigree frond, sensed through my hair. Pause at fibre on leaf. A soft puff to make it move.

As I respond to the specific qualities (structural, acoustic, atmospheric) of a site, I consider myself to be in dialogue; internal (performer) with external (site/landscapes). As performer, 'tuning in' implies a notion of resonance. Opening up my awareness[2] to that which is within and surrounding the spaces, form emerges as I respond to the *inform*ation contained within the site with inner and outer awareness. Each space has its own presence and the capacity to reflect and reinforce vibrations, a direct link to musical resonance. The site and performer could be said to affect each other in sympathetic response.

I found myself echoing some movement material from the previous year's 'dialogue' with the pipes, including touching, tapping, clinging and pulling away from them; a history of responses. But a year later I saw and smelled the decay inside the Palm House and heard the sounds of the wind and birds outside afresh. As my attention shifted, so did my moods. I was aware of a new engagement with the ropes this time and found myself responding in particular to the knots. The first verbalisation was tentative almost strangulated. The voice was *a little voice... bound, tense*, energetically

2   For me 'awareness' includes: softening; breathing; opening the senses; a receptive state; an 'even, hovering attention' (a term used by a student who adopted this while watching me perform).

informed by the idea and actual quality of knotted rope. But the query in '*a disturbance there?*' was to imprint itself in Improvisation 3 as a resonance; a connection to the presence (in absence) of Lady Louisa.

Palm House: Improvisation 2

Arc, arch, architectural, swooping, soaring, confident, recoiling, wind caught in the voice and movement - a moment of harmony.

I continue to grapple with terms such as 'attention', 'attentiveness', 'awareness', 'noticing' and the subtle differences between them, but it is clear that the development of perceptual awareness is key to my process. To be in a receptive state is fundamental for improvisation. This is a state of 'being' rather than 'doing'. 'Deep Listening', a practice developed by musician/composer Pauline Oliveros, encourages noticing and accepting all sound without judgement, close and distant, harmonious and dissonant, as it enters and departs the widened perceptual landscape. Phrases used in this practice such as 'imagine the distance between your temples' led me to develop phrases such as: 'listen through the skin'; 'see through the soles of feet'; 'open ears, nose, pores, and the spaces within to that which is beyond' to provide perceptual challenges during my own practice. Here it would be appropriate to acknowledge PATRICIA BARDI's 'ACTIVE BREATH' as an influence too. I appreciate in this practice the strong element of 'playfulness', which for me is a fundamental component of improvisation.

In Improvisation 2, above, I began looking outside at the fountain and the water in the distance and I remember gradually drawing my attention towards the glass, 'listening' along the way, then through the glass until I was inside the space of the Palm House and occupying my own inner spaces. As I worked from the forms within the space, no sense of character emerged but my voice which was knotted and dissonant in Improvisation 1 became harmonious. I was caught by the sound of the wind, and took on its dynamic in a swooping, playful engagement of movement and sound together.

In site-responsive work I believe that part of what I do is 'articulate' the space and am interested in architect Bernard Tschumi's phrases, as discussed by Nick Kaye in *Site Specific Art* (2000: 44), 'to make space distinct' and 'to state the precise nature of space' . But much more than this is at play. What is contained within a site? How far does substance – brick, glass, metal, stone, wood – act as a depository of past in*form*ation? What traces are there to be picked up on? What social/cultural narratives are inscribed? In most of my practice I do not research the 'history' of buildings or outdoor sites beforehand. My intention and imperative is to respond in the moment to the substance and content of the place itself and the mood and atmosphere communicated to me by the spaces at a particular time. Working in the same site reveals how variables such as weather, light and plant growth significantly affect the atmosphere and my mood as performer. But just as an improvisation is informed by what is there, it is also informed by what has gone before.

Palm House: Improvisation 3

Palm. Palm of hands... then the other plant - sharper.
Restates its presence in my movement.
An mmmmm sound arises to take me out and up, up, through the expanses of
leaves to the expanses of glass above... the sun, the birds again... way outside
now... Outward gaze but inner eye ...
Listen with every fibre
Here, my space
Safe, a friend... and then...

A tiny disturbance within (trace of number 1?)
Vibrations – expressed – Lady Louisa?
Resonance. Utterances.
Schism.
Me, space, Louisa, flashes of past, then in the present again.

Back against the bark – feel it, the texture, solid now.
Lean to solid. Head to tree. Connect, connect.

I was in a familiar place, sitting under the big palm. I managed to clear my mind of thoughts. I sat and waited. What emerged? As I leaned back and felt the texture of the palm trunk on my head, on my hair, soft and firm, resilient, my attention was caught by the fan-shaped leaves. A trace of a past improvisation emerged as I felt the energy of the centre of a leaf connect with the palm of my hand. I felt vibrations, vocally instigated at first then becoming a somatic disturbance. Lady Louisa came to mind; a woman trapped. On reflection this was a trace and resonance from Improvisation 1. From the journal entry above it can be seen that the improvisation returned to the substance of tree bark, which afforded me a more grounded connection from which I began to work towards a sense of ending (considered again later in the chapter).

The overall experience in The Palm House was of variable moods triggered by different stimuli 'allowed in' as I shifted between different foci and levels of attention and awareness. The relationship with the place in the three spaces became clearer and more defined, even though I had not set up any structures for the improvisations in advance. Although fresh material emerged during these improvisations I was aware that I repeated 'strategies' from previous visits such as playing off the names of the plants and tapping on pipes. My journal entries refer to several types of 'trace', including traces of previous physical and vocal responses and even the suggestion of past lives rendered present. The disturbance felt in Improvisation 1 manifested itself in Improvisation 3 and, as I interpreted it, connected to the persona of Lady Louisa. On reflection this 'disturbance' may have developed from the immediate sense of enclosure that I felt on my first ever visit to the Palm House despite the expansiveness of the space and the light afforded by the panes of glass. This was then amplified by the 'knotted' energy drawn from the ropes; resonances of the past, impinging on or further *inform*ing the present.

Hermitage

On a smaller scale and constructed predominantly of wood, The Hermitage was in direct contrast to the Palm House as a performance site. Positioning myself in front of it, with an invited audience viewing from the far side of the lake opposite, it offered an exterior landscape for a fourth improvisation.

Started looking out
Birds, trees, sky, space – a vista
Air, wind, water
Listening, skin, skin receiving, back of skull receiving...

Fabric of the house
Oak scales, shape of roof and extensions
Reflection of audience
Wind-rippled water... cleared reflections
Oak, decayed, gnarled. Deep sound emerged
Bent over, difficult to walk, made way to the seat

Images in windowpanes – reading book, horse
Sense of finishing, looking at my hand

The improvisation outside the Hermitage revealed more threads and
some bizarre occurrences. I had only seen the building once before, briefly
and at a distance, enough to help me decide where to place myself and
my audience. I prepared for a fresh dialogue with this new site without
memory traces of other improvisations entering the domain. I experienced
a direct relationship, an organic connection, between my breath and the
air. I became increasingly aware of opening up all of my senses, feeling the
wind on my skin and through my pores, a tactile contact as opposed to the
auditory one in the Palm House.

As I understood it at the time, my awareness shifted between the macro-
scale of the external environment to the micro-scale of inner sensations,
mediated through the material structures. I was aware of receiving specific
impulses from a few images depicted in the windows that I noticed
fleetingly during the improvisation, but my movement also reflected other
'unnoticed' images, picked up perhaps subliminally. In coming to a sense
of ending, I remember looking into the palm of my hand, standing to one
side of the Hermitage. It was not until afterwards, when I examined the
building in more detail, that I saw the image of a hand, in a similar position,
in one of the panes of glass. No doubt 'palm' themes from the previous
improvisations had left their traces, but it was the specificity of the position
which surprised me.

Additionally, less predictable movement and vocal forms emerged. These
were not so much to do with the structures but more with my engagement
in 'being' and responding to inner impulses. I was physically prompted
by the gnarled oak, of which the building was constructed, to bend over
almost double. A slow walk from one end of the house became difficult and

as I concentrated on the walk itself and the sensory feedback in the body, a deep sound rumbled within me to which I gave utterance, disturbing in its power and emotional resonance for me as performer. I was not sure whether I uttered the sound or the sound uttered itself through me. This hunched figure and its deep voice was, to one member of the audience, resonant of a gardener figure or keeper of the summer-house, a 'character'. Was this an example of my dancing enlivening the place; of a thread of that place unravelling to meet me?

The notion of 'resonance' becomes more palpable as other things happen, beyond the formal: moods fluctuate; memories are triggered; emotions are experienced; 'characters' seemingly emerge from nowhere. Improvisation certainly challenges the performer to take seriously ideas that "come out of the blue". (Claxton, 1997: 13) One could argue that any live performance is improvisatory, even if the material is set or 'known', as it requires performers to be 'in the present moment' and there will be elements of the unforeseen. By its very nature improvisation is unpredictable as one enters a world of the unknown.

The polyrhythmic training of TAKETINA, which I find helpful in developing vocal play and improvisational skills, stresses the importance of 'giving oneself to the unknown', 'letting go' and 'entering chaos'. As an improviser one has to be comfortable with that. I particularly appreciate the notion of 'non-knowing' expressed by Gaston Bachelard in his introduction to *The Poetics of Space* (1994: xxxii-xxxiii): "Non-knowing is not a form of ignorance but a difficult transcendence of knowledge. This is the price that must be paid for an oeuvre to be, at all times, a sort of pure beginning, which makes its creation an exercise in freedom." Having 'a sort of pure beginning' relates closely to what I would describe as a 'state of readiness without expectation' that is required to improvise. Dance colleague Gill Clarke reflected that the skills involved are of "spontaneous composition and that requires a great level of training of levels of attention so that you can take in detail of the whole piece". (Pam Woods, interview with Gill Clarke, Dec. 2001).

Endings also require particular attention. One has to find the moment as the last impulse reaches a place of settlement. Something says not to take on any more impulses, but rest there. Finish. In all the above improvisations

I felt a strong sense of ending; a sense of completion. But as there is never really 'completion' perhaps 'cohesion' is more appropriate, as suggested by American performer Ruth Zaporah, who provides some insight in *Action Theater* (1995: 54):

> "As you improvise, you lay down stones of action. In a sense you create a path. You hold all the stones in your awareness and that awareness affects your current action. As long as you stay aware and remember the stones you've laid down, your current action can't help but be responsive and relevant to your previous actions. The whole thing will be cohesive. In a cohesive composition, inner and outer awareness work hand in hand. They release new material, and simultaneously examine the path that has been travelled."

Hazel Smith and Roger Dean (1997: 36) suggest that "besides training and experience, we need to take into account the mind-set of the performer(s) at the time of performance". Without doubt one's own state of being will affect the improvisation but a disciplined application of skills such as opening up perception, attention and awareness , 'listening' with the whole body, 'noticing' and self-witnessing helps prevent the performer becoming 'attached' to what they are doing. Zaporah (1995: 24) reminds us of the importance of 'listening' skills in improvisation:

> "Our mind shifts its attention from object to object in erratic and irreverent ways. We can move from thought to feeling to imagining to remembering to sound to thought to taste to vision to thought and on and on. The less we control and inhibit this movement and the more we watch and listen, the freer our minds are to play with this vast assortment. Thinking is too slow... When we are thinking – as opposed to listening to ourselves with less attachment and staying with each movement – we never get beyond ourselves and the familiar."

As experienced in my own work, fully engaging in the quality of the movement and vocal sound impacts on one's system as a performer. What comes into play? As RUDOLF LABAN suggests in *The Mastery of Movement* (1971: 22):

> "Each movement originates from an inner excitement of the nerves, caused by an immediate sense impression, or by a complicated chain of formerly experienced sense impressions

stored in the memory. This excitement results in the voluntary or involuntary inner effort or impulse to move."

Laban's writing, although first published in 1950, links to thinking among neurophysiologists such Edelman and Tononi (2000) and Damasio (2000) who shed light on consciousness as a process within the realms of imagination and feeling; in Damasio's words "how it may work so that we can 'feel' a feeling" (2000: 81). Working 'in the abstract' (concentrating on a formal property of the movement or sound itself) may well elicit an emotional resonance. In working thus, 'from the outside in', Laban's 'effort actions',[3] for example, manifest themselves, in practice, in what I would call energy states. These are quite often perceived as emotional even though the dancer may have no inner/emotional motivation. I would suggest that these energies fuel responses which have given characteristics, and are thereby suggestive of 'characters'.

Actual resonance occurs during vocalisation through vibrations fed back into the body, but in applying 'effort actions' to voice as well as movement, there is possibly a double impact and a greater potential for resonance to be felt as memories and connections are triggered by the qualitative choices made. It is perhaps unsurprising that feedback in the body triggers unexpected responses. Playing with vocal dynamics, pitch and tone, and applying 'space', 'time', 'weight' and 'flow' variables leads to some intriguing moments as 'characters' and narrative threads arise.

I found many connections to American choreographer DEBORAH HAY's practice while working with her on solo adaptations in SPCP[4] 2005 and 2007. This experience consolidated my own discoveries and also gave me new insights. Hay's notion of 'cellular body' made sense to me. It sets out to challenge what she calls "the tyranny of the three-dimensional body" through a practice guided by questions, such as: "What if every cell in my body all at once has the potential to invite being seen, getting what it needs, surrendering the pattern of facing a single direction?" The challenge for

---

3   See Rudolf Laban in the Glossary for more details.

4   SPCP: Solo Performance Commissioning Project, run by Independent Dance. I worked with Deborah Hay in two of these projects for International dance artists at Findhorn, Scotland in 2005 ('Room') and 2007 ('The Runner'). Participants engage in daily group and solo practice, working with a series of questions and are challenged to perceive 'body' as a 'cellular body' beyond a three-dimensional form.

performer (and audience) is to perceive 'space' and 'time passing' (for me this related to Laban's 'effort actions') while also practising a choreographic 'score'.[5]

'Falling Among the Nettles' (2003)

The Palm House improvisations came close to 'pure' improvisation, but for 'Falling Among the Nettles' ('Nettles') I expanded my site-responsive work to include 'memory as site', including 'object as site' and for this created 'scores', very open to begin with but gradually building in complexity. Steinman (1989: 77) suggests that improvisation is "a process by which the evolving nature of the world around and within the artist is revealed by their actions". I performed improvisations in five different sites over five consecutive days. Each site was chosen for its connection to actual sites which held significant memories from each of five decades of my life. For the first decade, for example, I chose a bluebell wood, where at age six I fell among nettles while attempting to pick a bluebell and got badly stung. Into this improvisation came specific memories of my grandmother symbolised by a feather duster, and on a branch I hung a blue ballet tutu which I had worn at that age and which had been cared for over the years by my mother, now deceased. My mood shifts were instantaneous and considerable as I came towards the end of the improvisation, image triggering memory, memory triggering voice; an interplay between past and present. It was at moments like these that I appreciated the role of self-witnessing (mentioned earlier) in maintaining an all-important performer detachment.[6]

Unpredictably one of the bluebells I picked just collapsed. The moment contained humorous sexual innuendo but with the 'backdrop' of life's sting in my mind, disappointment in its lack of perfection turned to a huge sense of 'let-down', experienced again and again as a young child. In a flash the light mood turned to despair. I was six again. I gave anguished voice to the sky. As a performer I

---

5   A score in this context is a series of structured moments built from suggestions, instructions or 'directives' which I set myself such as: working with a memory in mind; an intention to use an object; a spatial, movement or vocal idea or pattern; a pre-planned 'activity'. Scores could be seen as maps (of varying detail) for improvisation.

6   Deborah Hay (SPCP) would ask us to 'witness' ourselves with imagined multiple outside eyes projected through 360 degrees. This was to help us to avoid 'traps' (getting caught up in an idea or emotion from which it might be difficult to move on) while remaining present moment by moment.

kept my outside eye, tracking, listening, ready for the next cue. I noticed a filigree over-hanging branch with fresh buds. Springtime hope. Soothed, I looked beyond me and saw my blue dress hanging in the breeze. I found myself curtseying.

I found increasingly that I took traces of one improvisation into another, not necessarily by consciously 'holding all the stones' in my awareness as Zaporah suggests, but perhaps (expanding on Hay's notion of cellular body) more through cellular-body-mindfulness. I built a sixth cumulative piece for the studio, consciously extracting key moments from the material prepared for, and which developed out of working in, all five sites. Although some were derived from direct, sometimes quite emotional, experiences, I scored them so that I was still predominantly 'performing action', focusing on qualities defined by weight, space, time and flow. The intensity of this period of practice and the specific narrative threads within the material unsurprisingly held some powerful personal connections. Some were triggered by the voice itself as it resonated in the body. Others were less tangible. New connections occurred throughout the process, including during the final piece in its studio setting:

Then I bow my head down forwards letting the shawl unravel. I thread my arms through and make one last limping bird-like turn before drawing it out to my right and up vertically to its full length.

And in this simple action, while walking slowly forward, I looked up and to the right and felt vibratory feedback in the body, a stirring, a re-sounding perhaps, deep within:

I walk slowly forward holding it in my right hand at arm's length. I am walking holding my mother's hand. I let the shawl spiral down, placing my bare right foot gently among the folds as it continues to crumple. My foot receives the soothing caress of my mother as she 'dies'.

My intention throughout this final piece was to create movement, vocalisations and images that could resonate for an audience on many levels, not to tell *my* story but to offer inter-woven, non-chronological fragments, conveying moods, emotions and themes. When I performed 'Nettles' (in the UK and abroad) members of each audience said they saw themselves, their story through the performance. The process of 'Nettles' was deeply personal, but still aimed to achieve a balance of connection and detachment.

I have not tried to explain, but rather considered what might be 'at play' in the 'unknowing' state that improvisation affords us as performers. Picking up on traces and threads laid down in past improvisations, and allowing them to unfold in new ways in spontaneous composition/ choreography is part of the performer discipline of keeping connection with everything that is happening within the body and at the same time heightened awareness of everything around. Open awareness of it all, a state of being in the moment, a state of readiness without expectation is fundamental to the dialogue between internal and external worlds. The role of sound (sounds perceived and experienced aurally and physically as listener and 'utterer') could be seen as particularly significant as powerful triggers of mood, character, memory, and emotion in my improvisations, where temporality is also part of the complex layering. I propose that 'cellular-body-mindfulness', while paying particular attention to the sensory world of sound, moves towards a definition of the Resonant Body in site-responsive improvisation.

Dr. Pam Woods is an independent dance artist, choreographer and educator, currently part-time lecturer (Drama) at the University of Exeter.

Her particular interests include: improvisation; site specific and site responsive work; the role of perceptual awareness in performance; voice within dance; dance theatre; devised theatre. Pam obtained a PhD Performance Practice in 2003, (University of Exeter), which comprised ten major projects developed under the title 'Site as Source and Resource for Sounding Dance Improvisation'. In 2006 she was artist-in-residence at University of Tasmania, enabled by the Lisa Ullman Travelling Scholarship Fund. Pam is founder member of Exeter-based Dance-lab Collective (established in 2010), which investigates the process of collaboration.
p.g.woods@exeter.ac.uk

Bibliography

Bachelard, G. (1994) *The Poetics of Space* (trans. Jolas, M.), Boston, MA: Beacon Press

Claxton, G. (1997) *Hare Brain, Tortoise Mind*, London: Fourth Estate

Damasio, A. (2000) *The Feeling of What Happens: Body, emotion and the making of consciousness*, London: Vintage

Edelman, G. M. and Tononi, G. (2001) *Consciousness: How Matter Becomes Imagination*, London: Penguin Books

Hay, D. (2000) *My Body the Buddhist,* Middletown, CT: Wesleyan University Press

Kaye, N. (2000) *Site Specific Art*, London: Taylor and Francis

Laban, R. (1971/1950) *The Mastery of Movement*, London: Macdonald and Evans

Pearson, M. and Shanks, M. (2001) *Theatre/Archaeology*, London: Routledge

Steinman, L. (1986) *The Knowing Body*, Boston and London: Shambhala

Smith, H. and Dean, R. (1997) *Improvisation, hypermedia and the arts since 1945*, Amsterdam: Harwood Academic Publishers

Zaporah, R. (1995) *Action Theater: The Improvisation of Presence*, Berkeley, CA: North Atlantic Press

The Dwelling Body

Suze Adams

Abstract

'The Dwelling Body' is concerned with raising awareness of the interface between body and place and examines ways in which habitual responses might be disturbed using yogic breathing as a practice of attention. By focusing on abdominal breathing and the immediate landscape environment, the practitioner becomes a conduit of bodily sense. In this way, the author proposes that a bodily intelligence can be developed and a heightened awareness of the inter-relationship between body and place fostered over time.

The chapter draws on the rich concept of dwelling to explore and expand multi-sensory experiential understandings of the landscape of practice. Dwelling is translated as embodied potential where sustained attention to the phenomenological landscape can prompt alternative understandings of the experiential and, as a result, radically alter practice. Dwelling is therefore considered a formative state and is not aimed toward any predetermined end.

This chapter reflects the underlying knowledge that both body and place are continually in process and recognises the vital inter-relationship of place and identity – both in movement (active engagement) and in stasis (passive observation). The dwelling body delicately balances the lived with the learned – multi-sensory knowledge of the experiential landscape combining with conceptual understanding in the actuality of performative engagement through a merging of practical and theoretical considerations.

Images from the author's case study, 'Communion', are incorporated throughout.

Crater Loch

She stands erect on the shore;
sentient, exposed.
She is I ...

I came to Mull to pay homage to my maternal ancestors,
with a location for this quiet performance already in mind.
S'Airde Beinn, an extinct volcanic crater in the north-west of the island -
the family cairn situated close to the base of the mountain
marking the route from Dervaig to Tobermory,
the drovers' way, the funerary route.

S'Airde Beinn was one of my mother's favourite haunts
but it is a place that resonates in the present as well as the past;
it has its own power to enchant, to entice,
the water of unknown depth, the sky of unimaginable breadth.

I attune myself to the environment slowly,
take time to circle the lochan
sensitive to my intentions yet open to what I find;

the challenge of the elements, the cold of the water,
the intensity of exposure, physical and psychological.

I make my way to the far side,
to a finger of boulders that go down the inside the crater,
a spine of rocks that disappear into the lochan below.
I step into the water, straighten and close my eyes;
attending to breath and bodily balance,
feeling my way and, grounded through my feet,
straightening to the sky above.
Deep lungful of cool air, slow exhalation of warm breath.

Focusing on breath and posture, I open my eyes -
acknowledgement of a charged environment,
remembrance of my ancestors.

A practice of attention;
body, breath, location
flowing more keenly than before ...
the dwelling body is (im)placed,
I'm placed.

... She stands on the edge of the lochan;
her abdomen fills, and falls.
Eyes open, softly scanning, observing
ears attuned, sensitive,
following the direction of any resonance,
head tilting to locate the sound.

She feels the strength of the wind, the whip of the skirt against her legs;
she feels the chill of the water that gently moves at her feet.

She is calm; aware of the elemental pull,
the allure of this her ancestral meeting place.
She hears whispers on the wind, pays her respects;
a ritual prayer in celebration of those who have come before
and those who have yet to arrive.

"Dwelling is both a noun (the place to which one returns) and a verb (the practice of dwelling); my dwelling is both my habitat and my habitual way of life. My habitual way of life, ethos or set of habits determines my character (my specificity or what is properly my own). These habits are not given: they are constituted through the repetition of bodily acts the character of which are governed by the habitat I occupy".[1]

When working in the experiential landscape, it can be hard to know where to begin. How to find a way into a place? How to interpret the complex combination of corporeal and conceptual influences and references that simultaneously invade awareness? How to make sense of the elemental with the material, the felt with the seen, the intangible with the tangible? And how to articulate the sensuous geographies of place when time shifts, balance falters and awareness is constantly challenged? Questions of how to attend and how to respond are insistent. Yet by focusing on the inter-relationship between self and place and on connections between instinctive

---

1   Rosalind Diprose quoted in Meskimmon (2011: 19).

(habitual) embodied responses and the surrounding environment (habitat), I propose that it is possible to foster new understandings of the inter-relationship between body and place.

It is a matter of somehow adjusting accustomed responses, fracturing routine reflexes and radically readjusting environmental references so that the familiar becomes once again unfamiliar. In this way, the interface of body and place is sensitised and the relationship between them brought to the fore. It is a matter of paying full attention and shifting that attention away from the known, of refocusing embodied engagement and bodily posture, of (repeatedly) expanding awareness from body to place and from place back to body again... of dwelling simultaneously in the body *and* dwelling in place. As Boston-based performance artist Marilyn Arsem advises: "Pay attention to what you are paying attention to".[2] And I would add, then turn your attention to the overlooked and neglected, what you are *not* paying attention to.

One route into the immediacy of the experiential is to attend to the dwelling body, the situated body, through the breath. By focusing on abdominal breathing (following yogic traditions), a bodily intelligence can be developed and, over time, a heightened awareness of the inter-relationship between body and place fostered. Every breath we take is an exchange with our environment:[3]

Focus on the breath;
begin to centre the body within the landscape environment -
feel the weight of the body on the ground,
feel the surface of the land under the feet,
become aware of the materiality of place but
at the same time
pay attention to the fleeting,
to the elements, to the senses
and to glimpses of landscapes beyond.

---

2   Marilyn Arsem (Founder member of Mobius Inc, a Boston-based collaborative, and head of performance at the School of the Museum of Fine Arts, Boston) in a performance workshop at the Living Landscapes conference, Aberystwyth, June 2009.

3   A thoughtful reminder from yoga teacher Erica Cole.

Focus on multi-sensory awareness of the moment;
the tangible and intangible essence of embodied experience
where aspects of landscape and self
collude and collide.

The Dwelling Body describes a form of embodied inhabitation. Incorporating yogic breathing exercises and poses into a practice of attention, the dwelling body constitutes a (temporary) immersive engagement, a form of dwelling in the landscape. The dwelling body is founded on an understanding of the etymology of the verb 'to dwell'. According to phenomenological philosopher Edward S Casey (1993: 114)

there are two roots to the verb dwell: the Old Norse *dvelja:* to linger, delay, tarry and the Old English *dwalde:* to go astray, err, wander. But how is it possible to linger *and* to wander, how might one delay *and* go astray?

Building on the twin roots of the word, dwelling translates in practice as *the mobilised body* – a body that wanders but also lingers in the landscape, a body that attends to the environment and responds spontaneously in postures still and/or moving but always centred and sensitive to the multi-sensory. Imagine the body as a tree for a moment: a tree rooted but swaying in the wind, accommodating birds and small animals, nourishing the growth of plants such as ferns and lichens, absorbing carbon dioxide, giving oxygen... and then the body, your body, immersed and interacting in the environment, both *apart* (with its own distinctive character) and, importantly, *a part of* the landscape. And yet, the dwelling body resides in movement as well as stasis... is grounded yet retains its mobility and an awareness of other dimensions, expanded sensually and conceptually in attentive practice; rooted but not static.

In this chapter I approach the experiential landscape with an understanding of dwelling as a concept that moves with the body, in time and in place. Viewing the landscape of everyday practice as a locus of dwelling assumes an understanding of dwelling as a bodily state where multi-sensory experience and meaning emerge via active engagement as well as passive observance. Dwelling is understood here as a formative state and not aimed toward any predetermined end. As such, dwelling is understood as *potential* – the result of located engagement generated by a series of unforeseen encounters and passive *as well as* active engagement.

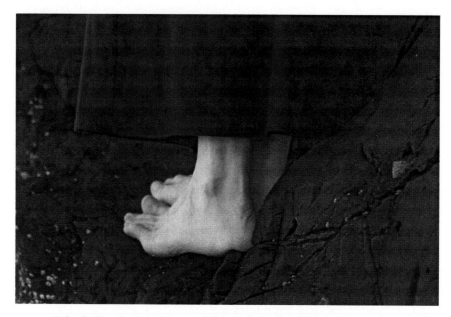

"...both the continuing accessibility and the familiarity of a dwelling place presuppose the presence and activity of the inhabitant's lived body. This body has everything to do with the transformation of a mere *site* into a dwelling *place*. Indeed, *bodies build places*." (Casey, 1993: 116)

As Casey underlines here, a dwelling approach resonates with thoughts of embodiment as well as with inhabitation of place, containing echoes of identity and intimacy (physical and psychological). An awareness, simultaneously, of dwelling in place and dwelling in the body; an awareness of movement and stasis, of constancy and transience, with dwelling understood as action and inter-action as well as passive immersion.

Yet, if the word dwelling is to be adopted in order to convey a definitive approach to the experiential landscape, as a way of reading and relating self and place, there is a need to consider further terminological associations and philosophical precedents. I refer specifically to philosopher Martin Heidegger (1975: 145) who asks the question: "what is it to dwell?"

Heidegger writes:

"We are attempting to trace in thought the nature of dwelling...
The real dwelling plight lies in this, that mortals ever search anew
for the nature of dwelling, that they *must ever learn to dwell*." (*ibid*:
145)

This I believe is the crux of a dwelling lens – the learning to dwell of the situated body where attention to the breath has the potential both to ground and to engage the body in and with the immediate landscape in movement and in stasis. In practice, when attention is focused on the localised particularities of place, dwelling can be continually learnt anew. In this respect, dwelling is continually revitalised and reinvented and retains the *potential* to offer new understandings of the inter-relationship between a self and a place. Such understandings necessitate reassessment of the familiar landscape of practice. They can also prompt engagement with specific landscape locations where such concepts can be explored and challenged through direct engagement with the immediate environment.

A practice of attention;
body, breath, location.

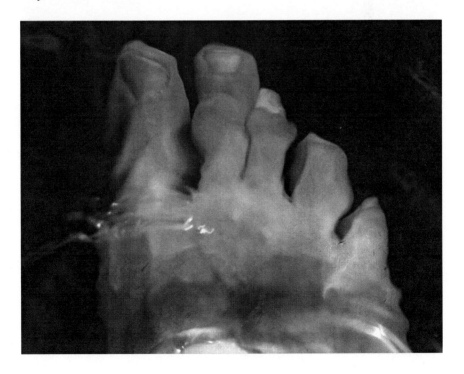

"When I inhabit a place – whether by moving through it or staying in it – I have it in my actional purview. I also hold it by virtue of being in its ambiance; first in my body as it holds onto the place by various sensory and kinaesthetic means, then in my memory as I "hold it in my mind." ... holding onto a place so as to prolong what I experience beyond the present moment. In this way, place and self actively collude." (Casey, 2001: 687)

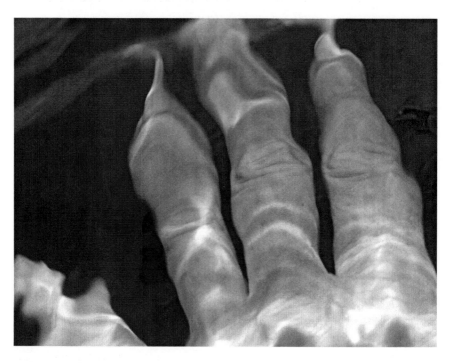

Casey's words here emphasise the relationship between movement and stasis when seeing the body through a dwelling lens, where a place is *inhabited* either 'by moving through it or staying in it'. This evocation of the inter-relationship between self and place is complex and yet when translated into situated practice can both instruct and reward. Focusing on the breath, the dwelling body responds to the immediacy of the landscape encounter and holds the potential for an expansion of awareness and the development of a bodily intelligence.

Film theorist Vivian Sobchack (2004: 1) asks what it means to be embodied and questions how the lived body might be implicated in making 'meaning' out of bodily 'sense'. This is an issue that is directly pertinent to our consideration of a dwelling lens – that is, a performative interpretation of the experiential where the body itself acts as a conduit for a multitude of affective triggers and sensory registers. Here, the making of 'meaning' out of bodily 'sense' is of paramount importance if performances and artworks are themselves to embody echoes of the lived and reach beyond the anecdotal to touch receptive audiences or to encourage collaborative practice.

Sobchack writes of her approach as not seeking 'essences' but instead "the meaning of experience as it is embodied and lived in context" with "meaning and value emerging in the *synthesis* of the experience's subjective and objective aspects" (*ibid*: 2, italics in original). As such, the 'synthesis' that Sobchack identifies is key to understanding the dynamic role of the body in my exploratory practice where attention to the breath concentrates focus and helps encourage alternative embodied understandings and perspectives on place. In such a way, new perceptions, understandings and interpretations of the relationship between self and place can potentially be explored.

Here the body is recognised as a site of cross-fertilisation for a multiplicity of influences and references (lived and learned, instinctive and habitual, practical and theoretical). In this respect, the practitioner becomes a conduit of 'bodily sense' within which a range of multi-sensory observations are experienced. Such landscape encounters are in turn bodily reconfigured in a 'synthesis' of the corporeal with the conceptual as a result of embodied engagement – the culmination of a range of responses to the experiential landscape that have the potential to both inform and transform practice. It is this interpretation of bodily 'synthesis' that underpins a dwelling lens, an understanding that both inspires and guides my approach (as well as critical response) to the landscape of practice – as, for example in *Communion*, the case study evidenced in this chapter.

To return to the "making of meaning out of bodily sense", Sobchack (*ibid*: 179) proceeds to consider the relationship between "subjective imagination" and "objective imaging". This is, of course, particularly relevant in practice when the performativity of embodied engagement plays a significant role in the analysis and development of projects and project outcomes. In my experience, it is in the act of performance that critically informed intentions give way to spontaneous improvisations and that earlier practical intentions (or previously adopted methods) are adapted in attentive response to the immediacy of the experiential landscape.

It is, as such, in the process of embodied exploration that the subjective and objective aspects of practice might merge and, importantly, where new understandings and interpretations might emerge. Pragmatic *and* intuitive, aesthetic *and* strategic decisions are constantly processed and re-processed by the body in response to the immediacy of affective experience through a complex (conscious and unconscious) cross-fertilisation of influences and references. When the bodies of others enter the process through the act of collaboration, this merging becomes both more complex and more comprehensive.

In *Is Any Body Home?*, Sobchack investigates our connectedness to our bodies and says that she understands "our *ontological* relation to our bodies as rich, ambiguous and multidimensional", adding that "both empirically and philosophically our bodies are the essential premises of our being in the world" (*ibid*: 182). Here Sobchack considers our bodies themselves as dwelling places, effectively our bodies as our first home – indeed, it is as such that our bodies can help make 'meaning out of bodily sense' and deepen an understanding of the relationship that exists between self and world. As Sobchack observes, "our corporeal materiality always ultimately grounds us even as it allows us to continually displace, disassemble, and reassemble ourselves" (*ibid*: 188).

A bodily grounding in place is vital to my practice. The material specificity of place, in the case study detailed here the rural landscape of Mull, becomes a pivotal anchoring point for exploration and examination of abstract concepts and elemental observations in practice. Perhaps such bodily grounding might also serve as a reminder that our bodies are not only efficient machines and useful tools but are also "sense-making sites for constituting meaning and realising both ourselves and a world" – thus serving to highlight the affective and multi-faceted nature of the inter-relationship between a body and a place (*ibid*: 190).

A dwelling lens follows a multi-sensory trajectory and reflects lived experience as perceived through, and performed by, the body in specific landscape locations. Consequently it should be understood that the performances I make and the artworks I produce are assembled as a direct consequence of sustained attention and sensitivity to the specificity of place where the interplay of body and place is key to understanding (and to the subsequent interpretation of) the world in practice.

As we have seen, the dwelling body becomes a site of cross-fertilisation for a multiplicity of influences and references – integrating the physical with psychological and the tangible with the intangible. However, it should be remembered that perception of the immediate landscape situation is affected by memories of past encounters and intimations of imminent futures where received knowledge, assumptions and familiarity with previously experienced landscapes are all challenged. The abrasive tension of a variety of competing issues blurs the boundaries between past and present, practice and theory, place and self as the body performs place and various affects seep and assimilate in and through the body. In this way, new understandings and enhanced practice can hopefully emerge.

As phenomenological philosopher Tamsin Lorraine suggests, there are intimations of:

> "... how the body comes into play in the production of the knowledges that inform our self-understanding and our conceptions of what is desirable as well as what is possible for human relationships and ethical community..." (Lorraine, 1999: 4)

Deep lungful, slow exhalation,
the body, the landscape.
Pay attention
to what I am paying attention to ...

Building on the twin roots of the verb to dwell and comprehension of the body as our first home, a dwelling lens reflects an understanding of place as process; the landscape as continually in flux, evolving continually together with, and alongside, myriad competing forces – human and non-human, elemental and geological, natural and cultural. Human geographer Doreen Massey (1994: 168) writes of the specificity of place as being in part formed out of the individual and particular "interactions which occur... (nowhere else does this precise mixture occur)" and in part due to "the meeting of those social relations... (their partly happenstance juxtaposition)" which 'produce' new effects and affects.

The conceptualisation Massey offers is of place as *process* – of the complex co-constituency of people and place and the underlying relationship of environment to identity (individual, social, cultural). Massey's comment on the 'happenstance' parallels my understanding of the value of chance encounters in the landscape, of affective injunctions and temporal disjunctions, and how these contribute to a continual reawakening and reconfiguring of the (transitory) relationship between a self and a place (where both – self and place – are continually in process).

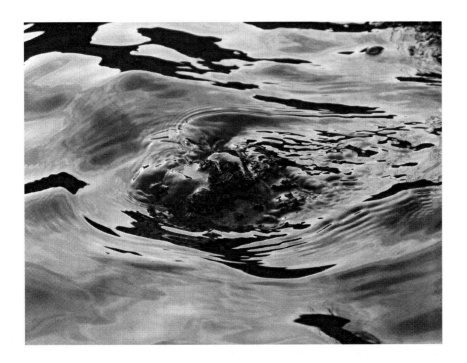

"Under fortuitous circumstances, the good humour of
enchantment spills over into critical consciousness and tempers
it, thus rendering its judgement more generous and its claims less
dogmatic. I pursue a life with moments of enchantment rather
than an enchanted way of life. Such moments can be cultivated and
intensified by artful means. Enchantment, as I use the term, is an
uneasy combination of artifice and spontaneity." (Bennett, 2001:
10)

A dwelling lens reflects the understanding of political theorist Jane
Bennett (above) in recognising the power of enchantment. Bennett's
acknowledgement of a calculated complicity between artifice and
spontaneity (as a way of echoing and sustaining the enchantment) is
reflected in my experience and understanding of the landscape of practice.
It also influences my understanding and interpretation of embodied
dwelling where, in practice, there is a delicate synthesis of the corporeal
and conceptual and the balance between control and abandon becomes
instructive.

The dwelling body gives equal weight to the lived and the learned – multi-sensory knowledge of the experiential landscape merging in embodied practice with conceptual understandings. The dwelling body balances the tacit and the explicit, the tangible with the intangible, in the actuality of the direct encounter. The dwelling body embraces the complexities, challenges and tensions of the world and, echoing the sentiment of Bennett, celebrates the power of enchantment as it balances precariously between spontaneity and artifice.

S'Airde Beinn is one of my favourite haunts,
a place that resonates in the present as well as the past;
it has its own power to enchant, to entice,
the water of unknown depth, the sky of unimaginable breadth

Dr Suze Adams explores the inter-relationship between people and place, examining connections between an experience of landscape and the forces (human and non-human) that shape the environments we encounter. Focusing on temporality and an oscillation between presence and absence in the experiential landscape, Suze's work slips a delicate veil between the physical and psychological, documentation and poetry, fact and fiction. Her practice presents in the form of still and moving imagery, sound, text and performance and often incorporates objects in order to allude to other times and places.

Drawing on a range of multi-disciplinary references, her research critically examines the concepts of dwelling and home, where dwelling is understood as ontological and home as non-unitary. Located between description and analysis, her work raises questions around issues of belonging and identity, about what and where we might call home.

Suze is an independent research artist who exhibits/performs across the UK and Europe. She is a founder member of Space Place Practice and part of the Family Ties Network.
www.suzeadams.co.uk
www.space.uwe.ac.uk
familytiesnetwork.wordpress.com

Bibliography

Bennett, J. (2001) *The Enchantment of Modern Life*, Oxford: Princeton University Press

Casey, E. (2001) 'Between Geography and Philosophy', *Annals of the Association of American Geographers*, Volume 91:1, 683-693

_____ (1993) *Getting Back into Place,* Bloomington, IN: Indiana University Press

Heidegger, M. (1975) *Poetry, Language, Thought,* New York: Harper and Row

Lorraine, T. (1999) *Irigaray and Deleuze: Experiments in Visceral Philosophy,* New York: Cornell University Press

Massey, D. (1994) *Space, Place and Gender,* Cambridge: Polity Press

Meskimmon, M. (2011) *Contemporary Art and the Cosmopolitan Imagination,* London: Routledge

Sobchack, V. (2004) *Carnal Thoughts,* Berkeley, CA: University of California Press

THE VOCAL BODY

Konstantinos Thomaidis

Abstract

In current understandings of voicing, especially in long-standing training formulae for actors and singers, the body is considered as a supporting *mechanism*. Good, healthy and aesthetically pleasing voice is produced when all the relevant body parts function efficiently. Still, this chapter asks: is the mechanistic paradigm the only option? Can we decisively map our physiology into apparatuses that contribute to sound-making and parts that resist participation in voice or stay unaffected by sounding? What are the consequences of such a paradigm for both the extra-daily and the everyday voicers?

Drawing on his work as a movement specialist and director with experimental opera groups which seek to challenge the body-voice dichotomy (Experience Vocal Dance Company and Opera in Space) as well as his doctoral project on the physicality of the voice in vocal dance, post-Grotowskian practitioners and Korean *pansori* singers, the author shares his observations on the possibilities of physiovocal unity. Using a practical session with opera singers as a case study, he foregrounds an integrative perspective, which moves beyond understandings of the body as a mere facilitator or homebase of vocal emission.

"...voice training should always be preceded by integrated body training...
Voice and speech training is body training..." (Lessac, 1997: 17)

The ephemerality and contingency of the voice has instigated two main tendencies in its theorisation. Since linguist Ferdinand de Saussure's "phonic but incorporeal" signifiers (1959: 118), logocentrism, founded on a model whereby signifiers effect the communication between signifieds, has seen voice as a tool-to-be-forgotten in favour of the transmitted meaning. Psychoanalyst Jacques Lacan, on the other hand, connected voice to the drives and, in particular, to the invocatory drive, suggesting voice as one of the paramount incarnations of his *objet petit a*, the object-cause of desire, that which is a void and at the same time that which can fill the void (Harari, 2004: 110-11; Žižek, 1992: 4). The voice, as something always-already missing, is at the centre of Michel Chion's analysis of the *acousmêtre*, the outside-the-frame cinematic voicer (1999: 129). Similarly, critic Steve Connor formed an analysis of the 'vocalic body' as the body source to which a voice is attributed. This source is reconstructed and/or produced by the listener, as it is already absent when the voice is perceived (2001: 35-43).

Theatrical performance, however, provides a unique vantage point for a discussion of vocal presence. Few theorists have worked in this direction: Barthes applied Kristeva's distinction between the geno-text and the pheno-text to his understanding of singing; he thus refers to the *pheno-song* (the 'surface' of the song, its notational codes and particular style) and the *geno-song* (the production and articulation of sounds that reveal the direct connection of the voice to the material, bodily mechanisms which give birth to it). It is here, in the realm of the geno-song, that Barthes discovers the possibility that the voice can achieve a corporeal presence, what he names "the grain of the voice" (1977: 181). This 'grain' is the manifestation of the aspects of physicality engaged in the production of spoken or sung utterances, the bodily trace that seals each voiced emission in such an unrepeatable way that the voice becomes a direct allusion to the unique body that made its genesis possible in the first place. The 'grain' is what allows the listener to distinguish between this or that singer. More recently, Adriana Cavarero, Italian philosopher and feminist thinker, criticised the strategies with which Western philosophy has deprived *logos* (≈ discourse or reason) of its voice, turning it into an abstract, non-audible contemplation, and reclaimed the "uniqueness of the voice" (2005: 11).

Building on my case study, I will examine the workings of this bodily anchor of the voice. More specifically, I will trace how the body is shaped through systematised voice pedagogies. My attempt will be to scrutinise not only the 'unique voice' or 'grain' of each particular performer, but also the collectively aspired/imagined/cultivated uses of the body/voice promoted within systems or traditions, a concept and praxis for which I employ the term 'vocal body'.[1] In other words, I will not focus on G. and D. as individual singers only but also as trained opera singers. Similarly, J. will be seen as an example of a trained actor/voicer too.

This is the first day of work with a collective of young professional opera singers. They are rehearsing towards a modern staging of a Baroque oratorio. Their concept involves choreographed movement, development of characters through stylised physicality and audience immersion. As their experience in movement-based acting is rather limited, I have been invited by G., the company's soprano, to lead a series of related workshops with them. My briefing before the session is short but informative: "Feel free to explore movement ideas, but do not try to mess with our voices".

The training of the operatic vocal body can be seen as a case of objectification. In the world of *bel canto*, the voice needs to exhibit defining characteristics (the *chiaroscuro* or 'light-and-dark' quality of harmonics and the seamless blend of registers), which are achieved through scientifically informed strategies (*appoggio* breathing and stroke of the glottis). Similarly, opera singers are trained less as voicing subjects and more as voice types, each one of which is expected to guarantee maximum efficiency in performance and optimal quality of the vocal instrument for a long-spanning career.

The training of *bel canto* acquired its original shaping and formulaic codification between the seventeenth and nineteenth centuries. According to theoretical physicist Basarab Nicolescu, this is the period when the split originated between subject and object in the first formulations of modern science (2008: 13). In fact, the training of the classical singer grew hand in hand with advances in the study of anatomy and physiology. It thus comes as no surprise that the most celebrated voice teacher of the heyday of nineteenth-century *bel canto*, Manuel Garcia II (1805-1906), is also credited with the invention of the laryngoscope (1855). Mathilde Marchesi (1821-1913), another well-known voice tutor, used to declare

1   To my knowledge, the term 'vocal body' has been used interchangeably with the term 'breath body' by Experience Bryon in her rehearsals with Vocal Dance Company to allude to the connection of the voice and movement through the pelvic girdle and the isolated use of the iliopsoas muscle. I deliberately see this as one of the possibilities of breath/body integration and apply the term more widely to the (discursive and practised) unity of physicality and voice in other training systems too.

that "...scientific knowledge is indispensable to professors of singing, because it enables them to treat the vocal instrument in a natural and rational manner" (1970: xiv). Elsewhere she goes as far as to claim that "there are only two Vocal Schools in the whole world: the good, from which the best results are obtained, and the bad, in which the reverse is the case" (Marchesi, 1970: xviii). From Marchesi's oft-quoted maxim to James Stark's recent affirmation that "[v]oice scientists, too, recognize that classical singing techniques offer the most elegant and sophisticated use of the voice" (1999: xii), the pedagogy of *bel canto* has revolved around the postulate that its methodologies and aesthetics are corroborated by hard science. It is precisely this belief that makes opera singers, such as G. or D., experience alternative routes to voicing as 'messing' with a tool that has been scrupulously harnessed over a long training period.

When I arrive at the rehearsal space, G. and D., the company's alto, are warming up. I decide to observe for a while. They are both standing almost immobile next to the piano, each with palms placed on their lower ribcage, which hardly seems to move even though they sing rather long and intricate passages. From time to time, D. places her index finger in front of her lips and repeats a phrase if she judges that too much out-breath has been expedited. G. uses her palm to ensure that either there is vibration on the top of her cranial structure or that her jaw and back of the neck remain unaffected in the higher register.

Optimal breathing for the opera singer invites the practice of *appoggio*. The word derives from the Italian verb *appoggiare*, meaning 'to lean on'. The term refers to the control of the antagonistic functions of the inhalatory and exhalatory muscles. After a quiet inhalation, the singer engages the intercostals and lateral abdominal muscles and maintains them in the shape they have acquired during inhalation (lowering and expansion) even during voicing. The resistance against the upward and inside recoil of the breathing muscles is a deliberate manipulation of the physiology so that "all notes, from the lowest to the highest, are produced by a column of air over which the singer has *perfect command*" (Lamperti: 22; emphasis added). The maintained expansion of the lower ribcage and the *rectus abdominis*, commonly tested through tactile observations as with G.'s 'hugging' palms, requires from the singers "the greatest degree of torso stability" (Miller, 2004: 3). This is why D. and G. stood in perfect alignment while warming up or felt more confident when their torso was relatively intact when moving. The resulting immobility of the torso, which also bears the imprint of neo-classical aesthetics (exemplified in the Greek sculptures of *kouroi*) in the genesis of opera, is known in the operatic world as the 'noble posture' (Jacocks, 2007: 64; Striny, 2007: 20).

Yet another core concern of *bel canto* pedagogy is the forceless, imperceptible use of the notes that lie in the points of transition between the registers – the points, commonly called 'breaks', where for a non-trained singer, such as J., the voice quality alters drastically (Stark, 1999: 58-73). Traditional *bel canto* training categorises performers in specific voice/character types and addresses the 'problem' of the breaks in a manner specifically targeted at each voice-type (Knapp, 1972: 83-88; Miller, 2004: 129-68). This categorisation is known as *Fach*, from the German word that translates as 'pocket' or 'case'. In a sense, the operatic singer is 'pigeon-holed' in terms of their range, timbre, volume and even character. However, recent research reveals that *Fach* is more of a cultural precept than an anatomical fact. While it is true that "the predominant range of an individual's voice is predetermined by the anatomy of the vocal mechanism" (Davies and Jahn, 2004: 9), the same laryngologists forewarn that "such classifications should only be regarded as a guide and are artificial" (2004: 13). It is then the pedagogical environment and choices made by the teacher(s), as well as the trainee's individual aesthetics and aspirations, that contribute considerably to the final range employed by the voicer. Put differently, even the customary division between soprano (G.), alto (D.), tenor, baritone and bass (J.) voices is, to a certain extent, an outcome of the disciplinary workings of *bel canto* pedagogy upon the vocal body rather than a physiological given.

Soon J. arrives. He is the actor who will perform the role of the narrator, but will also sing the bass line in the choruses. After a series of yoga- and t'ai chi-inspired sequences designed to unite movement and breath, I invite all three to pick their favourite part of the space and to stand, sit or lie in a comfortable position. With their eyes closed, I guide them through a body scan. The purpose is simply to bring their mind's eye to each body part, starting from the toes and moving slowly all the way to the top of the head, while imagining that breath happens in every area of the body. "How does your left heel breathe? Can you inhale and breathe out through your right armpit? Now, can you allow each out-coming breath to translate into sound?"

The exercise runs for a short while. J. is quite at ease with my instructions. He lies on the floor and seems to experience joy in turning each of his body parts into a distinct vocal character. His voice constantly changes and, while exploring breathing into his right shoulder blade, it glides upwards and breaks, making a squeaking sound. G. looks comfortable in producing sound. There is, however, an apparent disconnection between her imagination and voicing; she indicates to me that she is breathing in/to different body parts by slightly tensing them, but her attention is on her diaphragm. She is still standing with her hands 'hugging' her lower ribs and her voice remains unchanged throughout the exploration. "Watch your voice, J.", whispers D., who has rather unwillingly followed his example and tries lying on the floor. D. seems confused about the exercise. She starts in a vein similar to G.'s. She even opens her eyes and takes swift looks at her different body parts. At a certain point, she looks around and quickly drops her hands to the sides of her body in response to G.'s stiff stance and begins imitating J.'s sounds.

In comparison to the two opera singers, who have absorbed and embodied the operatic vocal body and its fixed, advocated-as-optimal mechanics, J. is more willing to experiment and discover. Does this mean, however, that he breaks free from any notion of a collectively trained vocal body? J., as an actor trained in a highly acclaimed UK drama school, exhibits the vocal body practised by such advocates of the 'natural' voice as twentieth-century speech trainers Cicely Berry, Michael McCallion or Patsy Rodenburg. Anatomically, this is a development of the normal breathing cycle, relying on the downward movement of the diaphragm for increased capacity of inhalation and the upward movement of the abdominal wall and the intercostals for relaxed out-breath.

In this strand of work, the voice is understood as being affected by the intimate connection between the trainees' physicality and their psyche (Berry, 1997: 26; Linklater, 2006: 7-11; Lessac, 1997: 13-17; Rodenburg, 1997: 38-40). The pedagogues' task is to facilitate a process

of *deconstruction*. In other words, they work having this basic principle
in mind: growing up in the West is a process of disconnection from one's
body and of accumulation of psychological traumas and cultural influences,
a process of disengagement with the self, which becomes obvious in the
limits and tensions one thinks of as inherent in the voice. Speech training
therefore becomes a process of doing away with the cultural encrustations.

The tool to achieve this is the well-respected remedy of relaxation and
effortlessness. First, especially when assimilating new breathing experiences,
the student relaxes and attempts to work without unwanted effort, locating
tensions and consciously experiencing the sensation of relaxation in the
body (Berry, 2000: 52; McCallion, 1988: 22). The suggested internal scan
in the working session is something J. is likely to have experienced as part of
his training, which can account for his eagerness to perceive and explore his
vocal body from the inside out. The student is subsequently taught the right
balance between relaxation and "energy in the muscles [of articulation]
themselves" (Berry, 2000: 22) and must, finally, get used to performing
without the usual effort. The right combination of precise muscularity and
relaxation can act as a safety net for the voicing performer, leaving space
for both conscious control and artistic flexibility – what McCallion would
describe as "the good use of the self" (1988: 125).

On one hand, the 'natural' vocal body contrasts with the operatic one in
that it encourages a subjective approach to the voice, rooted in a somatic
rediscovery of the body-self. Linklater acknowledges as the ultimate
objective of her training that students should "become very good, very
exciting, very idiosyncratic actors" (1997: 11). This justifies J.'s apparent ease
in creating surprising, characteristic, idiosyncratic sounds. 'Idiosyncrasy'
is key in understanding what the 'natural' voice pedagogy aims at when
encompassing aspects of the performer's bodily, psychic and emotional
resources. 'Good performer' equals 'unique (therefore employable)
performer'.

Still, even a pedagogy that promotes a 'naturally' free vocal body
and produces idiosyncratic/individual/unique voices, is a well-defined,
ideologically charged disciplinary training. Berry, McCallion and Linklater
have worked for educational institutions and vocational programmes
that prepare actors for the needs of the UK/USA market (CSSD and

RSC, RADA, LAMDA and Columbia University, respectively). Their training activities can be seen as pertaining to the 'atomist' or 'individualist naturalism' which prevailed in the UK/USA social sciences in the period after the Second World War. According to historian and philosopher Ronald Inden, 'atomist' or 'individualist' are the theoretical systems that privilege the individual over the collective, while approaches which claim that knowledge in social sciences can and should resemble knowledge in natural sciences are 'naturalist' (1995: 2-3). In the light of Inden's analysis, pedagogues of the 'natural' voice, who also provide the student with anatomical/physiological 'data' and aim at the 'maximisation' of the trainee's potential, may nurture personal development but still adhere to a scientifically fixated vocal body, that is, not insignificantly, a marketable one.

In other words, while the operatic vocal body may be a product of demanding construction (objectification of the voice) and the natural vocal body may emerge through deconstruction (experience of the voice as subject), their underlying training principles are still inspired by an aspiration to optimal efficiency. The methodology employed in describing the vocal apparatus in both instances favours the distinction between three of its functions: breathing (frequently encountered as support), sound-producing mechanism, and voicing (speaking or singing, with a minor interest in other vocal phenomena). This tripartite structure reproduces a systemic understanding of the vocal body as a mechanical apparatus that can be disaggregated and later reassembled in order to function more efficiently. This understanding is closely linked to the prioritisation of reason promulgated by the Enlightenment and the subsequent functionalist ideologies with which the Industrial Revolution and the spread of capitalism surrounded the (measured, routinised and controlled) body.[2]

Is there then a way out of the paradigm of efficiency, either subjectively or objectively obtained? My suggested warm up, inspired by yogic and t'ai chi techniques, comes from my encounter with Asian perspectives on the vocal body, in particular the training of Korean *pansori* singers.

---

2   For recent works that expand on the interrelation between the body and the 'project of Enlightenment', refer to the cited work of Burt, Foster, Gould and, for the formation of an over-arching discourse on the trained and in-performance body, to the latest publications by Conroy and Evans.

In this codified genre, singers are trained to breathe through their lower *danjeon*, the part of the torso situated underneath the navel, by tensing their abdominal muscles and canalising the strength inwards. "[*P*]*aetsim*, 'abdominal force,'" connects the singer to "the fountain of life's primary energy (*ki*)" (Park, 2003: 198). *Ki* (or *Qi*) in traditional Asian philosophies is understood as much more than energy exerted on the musculature. It is rather regarded and lived as a cosmic force, a source of vitality that connects the body-mind with the world in a present-oriented manner. *Qi* is seen as flowing or travelling either through meridians (tao), *chakras* (tantra) or *danjeons* (t'ai chi).[3] Through this flow, the breath does not merely support voicing; rather, it becomes a concrete locus where the body, the voice and the cosmos are yoked together.

Moreover, the vocal body of *pansori* transcends the obsession with the healthy or 'good' use of the self. Contrary to the natural/free or operatic techniques where breath support meets a non-tensed larynx and produces relaxed voicing, in *pansori* the flow from the *danjeon* upwards is fiercely obstructed at the level of the glottis and the larynx tenses and rises. The anatomical components of the laryngeal box are trained to resist breath, before allowing it to escape violently towards the resonators. This results in a 'sorrowful', highly forced and muscular sound production, which has been widely related to the Korean ideology of *han*, a sentiment of grief developed through historical experiences of war, occupation and migration (Kim, 1996: 114; Pihl, 1994: 6). The vocal body in this instance does away with preconceptions of the natural or physiologically optimal and embraces permanent modification in accordance with the 'grieving' aesthetics of the genre.

When I sense that they have all completed a full-body 'breath and voice scan', I decide to play a game. G. is to mould D.'s body into different positions, while J. moves freely in the room. As he is confident enough with his physicality, I encourage him to play with jumps on the spot, slow melt-downs towards the floor, turns, huge leaps, walking or caressing the walls with his body. D.'s focus is double: she has to surrender to G. and adopt each position, but at the same time mimic with her voice J.'s movement. D. seems bewildered at the beginning, but gradually discovers a broad range of sighs, groans and shouts as well as fully sung

---

3   For a detailed discussion of *Qi* in performer training, see Barba and Savarese (1991).

phrases. For the short duration of the exercise, she eases into not controlling her sound. She even smiles while voicing.

Of course, G. is crucial in helping D.; being a singer herself, she avoids putting D. into positions where her torso is twisted or her diaphragm suppressed. I then move to the final stage of exploration for D.: I ask J. to 'mould' D., making it clear that he needs to avoid too much pressure on the lower ribcage, and G. to move around, while making shapes with her hands, fingers and wrists. Now D. is to sing her aria from the second act, following G.'s hand choreography. J. is boldly imaginative and playful while sculpting D.'s body; he makes her balance, roll backwards on the floor or even handstand against a wall. G., knowing the aria and its demands, creates visual stimuli for D.'s breaths. Her hands shape suspensions, dramatic punctuations and uninterrupted flows in the air. D. is much more confident this time. In the multiplicity of bodily stances she adopts and in the use of her voice as a means of constant communication with a partner, emerge moments that could be potentially useful for her character. Just before we take a break, she turns to me and says: "This is so much easier when you are not checking on your body all the time".

The final exercises, especially D.'s discovery of fresh vocal possibilities whilst relating her sound-making to her partners, bring yet another paradigm to the fore: the vocal body cultivated through the post-Grotowskian line of Polish practitioners. For example, the singing pedagogy in the Polish company Gardzienice (founded by Wlodzimierz Staniewski in 1976) is heavily influenced by Mikhail Bakhtin's notion of the grotesque, unfinished body, which celebrates its materiality and is in constant connection to the Other and the world (1984: 316-43).

In the basic stance adopted by the body in training, the lower part is grounded, with the knees bent, while the upper part is malleable, succumbing to the slightest impulses travelling through a relaxed and flexible spine (Staniewski and Hodge, 2004: 87). The pelvic area, understood in Polish as the cross, is slightly tilted forwards so that the small of the back is more easily 'offered' to partners in acrobatic sessions and, consequently, the weight shifts to the front, allowing more space for the downwards release of the abdominals. The mouth hangs open and, as a result, sound is mostly shaped in the resonating chamber of the mouth cavity. In singing, the larynx is lifted, not only because of the extreme openness of the jaw, but also because of the 'exhaustive' use of breath and the slight tilting of the head upwards that I have observed in many of the Gardzienice actors. The excessive use of the musculature of the throat is evident in the sounding inhalations and exhalations, which, at the same time, function as a realisation of the Bakhtinian concept of the interrelated body (which, for the Russian philosopher, is mostly exemplified in the actions of devouring and defecating).

All training activities of the company, underpinned by the principle of mutuality (connection and interdependence), unfold as choral encounters within the ensemble and the slightest vocal or bodily impulse of one actor affects the others. In this sense, D.'s playfulness in the final section of the workshop did not derive from a different perspective on her mechanics of voicing, but from a solid focus outside herself. In Gardzienice, the musical depository of the company comprises mostly folk and liturgical songs and the score is very much open in rehearsals before any decisions are made about the final composition. Given that in our rehearsal/workshop G., D. and J. were working with a canonical score and that this was a taster session in a new methodology, the most important step was the shift in the vocal body paradigm that D. experienced: a first glimpse that voice need not emanate from a strategically organised, but hermetically closed, voicing apparatus, but can be rooted in the live interactions with other voicing bodies.

Conclusion

In this chapter, in dissecting the worldview crystallised *in* the voice (phenomenology of voicing), rather than the worldview communicated *through* the voice (semiotics of the voice), I have attempted to challenge the certainty with which exponents of the predominant pedagogy advocate that "[i]t is shortsighted to say that differences in technical approach are all of equal merit. Some manoeuvres simply work better than others" (Miller, 2004: 210). A closer look at, and critical investigation of, voicing practices reveal that both practitioners and scientists tend to draw on their body-related findings with an aesthetic agenda at hand. This agenda is not as obvious as it may seem in many cases, especially for reasons of marketing the relevant publications or foregrounding a particular use of the voice within a given performance discipline. In Davies and Jahn's words, "structure and function are inextricably interrelated in the vocal performer's larynx" (2004: 31).

The vocal body is a lens through which the physiovocal tendencies promulgated by distinct performance practices can be linked to their historical contours and aesthetic objectives.[4] As I have shown, the optimal efficiency of *bel canto* and the naturalised UK/USA voice trainings are indeed culturally defined and attempts can be made to transcend their methodologies. My brief discussion of *pansori* foregrounded a pedagogical approach that privileges aesthetics over concerns with nature or science. At the same time, the vocal body cultivated in the practices of Gardzienice introduced a concept of radical novelty: vocal inter-corporeality. The shaping of the body that participates in the genesis of voicing is the indicator *par excellence* of which parameter has been the prioritised element in each system: the physiovocal self, the object body/voice, the aesthetic result or the lived encounter. The examples could be innumerable, depending on the lens used to analyse the (trained) body that produces the voice.

In our session, the usual point of entry, the self, was not denied, but slightly shifted. The *Qi*-based practice of breath claimed the voice as yet another way to integrate with the (training) environment. Similarly, the Gardzienice-inspired games saw other bodies, tactile or visual communication, movement and space as partners, as impulses impacting on or generating the voice. This approach avoided the fixation of the voice and embraced its ever-changing character. As I left the room, with detailed notes on the workings of the operatic or 'natural' vocal body in rehearsal, I felt that this was the direction I should explore further in upcoming sessions with the group. Since I realised that, however illuminating and body-anchored the very category of the vocal body may be, ultimately

---

4   Of course, the vocal body is presented here as a point of departure, as a category-to-be-used. A more nuanced and rounded analysis of my working session could be obtained if there was space to fully answer such questions as the following: How is one to treat J.'s 'natural' vocal body in subsequent rehearsals, when he will sing the operatic score of the choruses? Even if D. enjoys her new findings now, how will she later balance the operatic needs of the score with her willingness to be influenced by the group? Can anyone 'measure' beyond doubt whether D. and G. embody the operatic vocal body to the same extent?

I have to succumb to the resistance of my subject matter to conclusive definitions. Any voice, exhibiting the dialogue between its individual and collectively aspired vocal bodies, is never a *fait accompli*. It is a work in progress.

_____

Dr. Konstantinos Thomaidis recently completed his thesis on the physicality of the voice in codified trainings at the University of London. He has worked as a performer, director and movement director in Greece, Poland, the US and the UK. He has taught extensively at Royal Holloway and the University of Winchester, as well as the CSSD and the Aristotle University of Thessaloniki, Greece. He is the Head of Movement of Opera in Space and an Associate Artist of EVDC-UK. His peer-reviewed publications have appeared in *Theatre, Dance and Performance Training Journal* and *Platform*, and he is currently writing for *The Performativity of Song and Dance* and *Studies in Musical Theatre*.
kon.thomaidis@gmail.com

Bibliography

Bakhtin, M. (1984) *Rabelais and his World*, (trans. Iswolsky, H.), Indianapolis, IN: Indiana University Press

Barba, E. and Savarese, N. (eds.) (1991) *A Dictionary of Theatre Anthropology: The Secret Art of the Performer*, London: Routledge

Barthes, R. (1977) *Image Music Text*, (ed. and trans. Heath, S.), London: Fontana Press

Berry, C. (2000) *Voice and the Actor*, London: Virgin Books

_____ (1997) 'That Secret Voice' in Hampton and Acker (1997)

Bryon, E. (2012) 'From Walking to Talking to Cartwheels and High Cs: An Examination of Practice-Based Laboratory Work into Physio-Vocal Integration', *Theatre, Dance and Performance Training* 3.1.

Burt, R. (1998) *Alien Bodies: Representation of Modernity, 'Race' and Nation in Early Modern Dance*, London: Routledge

Cavarero, A. (2005) *For More than One Voice: Toward a Philosophy of Vocal Expression*, (trans. Kottman, P.A.), Stanford, CA: Stanford University Press

Chion, M. (1999) *The Voice in Cinema*, (trans. Gorbman, C.), New York: Columbia University Press

Connor, S. (2001) *Dumbstruck: A Cultural History of Ventriloquism*, Oxford: Oxford University Press

Conroy, C. (2010) *Theatre and the Body*, Basingstoke: Palgrave Macmillan

Davies, D. G. and Jahn A. F. (2004) *Care of the Professional Voice*, London: A & C Black

Evans, M. (2009) *Movement Training for the Modern Actor*, London: Routledge

Foster, S. L. (ed.) (1996) *Corporealities: Dancing Knowledge, Culture and Power*, London: Routledge

Gould, S. (1981) *The Mismeasure of Man*, New York: W. W. Norton

Hampton, M. and Acker, B. (eds.) (1997) *The Vocal Vision: Views on Voice by 24 Leading Teachers, Coachers and Directors*, New York: Applause

Harari, R. (2004) *Lacan's Four Fundamental Concepts of Psychoanalysis: An Introduction*, (trans. Filc, J.), New York: Other Press

Inden, R. (1995) 'Human Agency in the Social Sciences', pp.1-19, typescript.

Jacocks, K. (2007) *Anatomy of Bel Canto*, Bloomington, IN: Author House

Kim, K. (1996) *An Introduction to Classical Korean Literature: From Hyangga to P'ansori*, New York: M. E. Sharpe

Knapp, M. J. (1972) *The Magic of Opera*, London: Robert Hale

Lessac, A. (1997) 'From Beyond Wildness to Body Wisdom, Vocal Life, and Healthful Functioning: a Joyous Struggle for our Discipline's Future', in Hampton and Acker (1997)

Linklater, K. (2006) *Freeing the Natural Voice*, London: Nick Hern Books

_____ (1997) 'Thoughts on Theatre, Therapy and the Art of Voice', in Hampton and Acker (1997)

Marchesi, M. (1970) *Bel Canto: A Theoretical and Practical Method*, New York: Dover Publications

McCallion, M. (1988) *The Voice Book*, London: Faber and Faber

Miller, R. (2004) *Solutions for Singers: Tools for Performers and Teachers*, Oxford: Oxford University Press

Nicolescu, B. (ed.) (2008) *Transdisciplinarity: Theory and Practice*, New York: Hampton Press

Park, C. E. (2003) *Voices from the Straw Mat: Toward an Ethnography of Korean Story Singing*, Honolulu, HI: University of Hawai'i Press

Pihl, M. R. (1994) *The Korean Singer of Tales*, Boston, MA: Harvard University Press

Rodenburg, P. (1997) 'Re-Discovering Lost Voices' in Hampton and Acker (1997)

Saussure, Ferdinand de. (1959) *Course in General Linguistics*, (trans. Baskin, W.), New York: Philosophical Library

Staniewski, W. and Hodge A. (2004) *Hidden Territories: The Theatre of Gardzienice*, London: Routledge

Stark, J. (1999) *Bel Canto: A History of Vocal Pedagogy*, Toronto: University of Toronto Press

Striny, D. (2007) *Head First*, Plymouth, CT: Hamilton Books

Žižek, S. (1992) *Looking Awry: An Introduction to Jacques Lacan Through Popular Culture*, Cambridge, MA: MIT Press

The Musical Body

Devising a Choreo-Musical Interpretation for *Tierkreis* (1974-75) by Karlheinz Stockhausen

Franziska Schroeder and Imogene Newland

Abstract:

In this chapter the authors explore a practice-led approach to understanding the role of the body in music performance.

Many writers have discussed the body in music performance, in improvised music, as well as in electronic music. In this chapter the authors offer new modalities of reflection on the musical body in the interpretation of existing contemporary repertoire. Specifically, they discuss a re-interpretation of German composer Karlheinz Stockhausen's musical work *Tierkreis*. Through the development of a specifically physical approach to the performance, the authors investigate the intrinsic relationship between the body and the music and point to an under-explored modality, which is not a musical choreography but a choreography that is shaped through the musical body itself. It is a modality in which music itself propels forward choreographic ideas, the body becoming the driving force behind musical interpretation. The authors' thinking is influenced by Susan Kozel's understanding of performance as an ecosystem (Kozel, 2007) and framed within a subjective account of musical embodiment.

By merging theory with praxis the authors offer a deeper understanding of the role of the body in music performance and consider how such contributions might lead to new and exciting interpretive frameworks for existing musical repertoires.

A definite look of agreement begins our duet. Reaching out to touch our instruments for the first time, Franziska raises the bell of her saxophone to the crook of her neck, while Imogene's fingers rest gently on the surface of the keys of the piano.

In Taurus we stand apart, calmness pervading Imogene's playing with light skin-deep pressure and slow release of breath, while Franziska remains silent centre stage, sculptural and still.
Approaches to body relations and choreography in this melody were derived from Taurus's association with notions of love, protection, beauty, balance, gracefulness, indulgence and sensuality. The star sign is also linked to the body part of the neck and the throat.

A swift movement brings us back to back on the piano stool, representing the visual shape inherent in the zodiac sign of Gemini. The growing resistance between our bodies, connected through shoulder blades and small of the back, is marked out in a struggle for sonic dominance. Just like the star sign itself, the melody wants to be of a curious, active, expressive and playful nature.

A sharp turn outwards in opposite directions marks our shift away from contact with each other and into the sign of Cancer, which we play facing away from each other with our instruments positioned at right angles to our bodies, imitating the visual shape of the zodiac sign itself. In reflecting the sign of Cancer, we want to nurture and protect the sounds with our instruments and bodies.

Moving apart, Franziska plays Leo centre stage while Imogene sits still and silent. Sounds and the performative body in this melody attempt to represent the noble, the hero, the leader and the liar – traits associated with Leo's star sign. The strident and vain tones project forcefully, with a touch now firm and a breath that is strong and domineering.

Moving into Virgo, Imogene sustains a long B flat while Franziska directs her instrument inside the strings of the piano, inside the belly of the instrument, creating an interior resonance across the body of the piano. Approaches to sounds and body relations in this melody were inspired by Virgo's association with the body part of the belly and lower intestines.

In Libra our two performative bodies and sounds want to balance each other; expressive, extrovert and graceful melodies interchange with unexpected, yet subtle, dynamic changes in an attempt to find sonic balances, similar to the sign of Libra that displays symmetry and balance. This melody becomes a sonic balancing act between two female bodies engaged in a process of mutual seduction.

Turning away from each other and moving further apart, Franziska introduces Scorpio. The physical gestures of the piano sequence are marked silently by the pianist. Without touching the keys of the instrument, Imogene moves mutely, intensely and secretively in her gestural sequences, representing the inward, reflective but also the dark, aggressive and deadly nature of the star sign itself. The piano is sounded only briefly in the first and second repetition, returning to the mute movements of the pianist at the end.

Moving apart, literally like having been fired from an archer's bow, Franziska walks across the stage and stands with her back to Imogene as the optimistic, jovial and good-humoured melody of Sagittarius is encompassed over the full distance of the stage. Just like Sagittarius, this melody wants to be adventurous, free and playful.

In Capricorn our two musical bodies move close to each other, the austere melody and rhythm of the triplet figures intertwining the bodies' movements. Franziska becomes the disturber of flow, lacing her arm inside Imogene's elbow, both bodies pulling on and away from each other. In reflecting the star sign's association with notions of restriction, control, power and limitation, the two performative bodies want to restrain each other, each pull of the arm being informed by the shape of the melodies that the performers play. A rise in the melodic line urges each performer to pull the other's body toward her own..

Aquarius is a melody that, in the same way as the star sign itself, is marked by sudden changes. It is experimental, electrical and at times, psychedelic.

An abrupt stamp of the foot (the star sign of Pisces corresponds to the body part of the feet) leads the two performers into Pisces. In this short piece, Imogene walks across the stage, her walk tracing the imaginary shape of Pisces on stage. The melody alludes to notions of freedom, utopia and spirituality, like the zodiac sign itself.

Franziska walks slowly across the stage to join Imogene again on the piano stool, where we finally play the last zodiac sign of the circle of twelve – Aries. The sign's corresponding body parts are face and head and we thus play the piece with both of our heads as far downwards toward the floor as possible. The leaning forward and hunching of our backs creates the shape of the sign. The melody portrays passion, aggression, impulsion and noisy violence.

The work *Tierkreis* (1974-75) by German composer Karlheinz Stockhausen was originally written for 12 music boxes, which Stockhausen had built specifically for the piece by the Reuge Music Box Company. *Tierkreis* formed part of the composition *Musik im Bauch* (*Music in the belly*) for six percussionists and music boxes; a work premièred by 'Les Percussions de Strasbourg' in Royan, France in March 1975.[1] *Tierkreis* consists of 12 simple and short melodies, each melody representing one sign of the zodiac. On his inspiration for the work, Stockhausen states:

> "In inventing each melody I thought of the characters of children, friends, and acquaintances who were born under the various star signs, and I studied the human types of the star signs more thoroughly. Each melody is now composed with all its measures and proportions in keeping with the characteristics of its respective star sign, and one will discover many legitimacies when one hears a melody often, and exactly contemplates its construction..." (Stockhausen, 1975, Score Preface)

The work is intended as a cycle of musical formulae for the 12 months of the year and the 12 human types; it has been called a "melodic naïveté" in the form of a "cheerful, empty-headed little tune" (Kenyon, 1980: 78), as well as a "fairy tale for children" (Maconie, 1976: 322) and "[...] a ritual

---

1   See URL2 for information on the intricate and meticulous crafting and fine-tuning of the music boxes.

played out in Mexican Indian scenery" (Kurtz, 1992: 205). *Tierkreis* has proved to be Stockhausen's most popular composition (Deruchie, 2007). Stockhausen used 12 different tempi in the overall cycle of the work, and each melody centres around one single pitch of the chromatic scale, with Stockhausen's own sign of Leo being composed around the pitch A. The entire piece of the 12 melodies thus employs all 12 chromatic pitches of the Western tonal scale. In order to make the compositional structures clearly perceivable, the performer is asked to repeat each melody at least three times and to vary each melody by using different dynamics, changes in pitch register, or by re-dividing the melodic material between instruments or using different forms of articulation. The performer is encouraged to improvise around what is quite clearly notated in the score. The composer states that improvisation is encouraged as long as it aids in clarifying the inner structure of the melodies while bringing out their distinctive characteristics.

Stockhausen specifically wanted performances of his works to exhibit an intrinsic relationship between the body and the music, asking the musician to abandon his/her ego in search of a more 'pure' or 'truthful' creative state. At the centre of this belief was Stockhausen's love for the movements of the body in dance. Indeed he was known to say that part of a musician's regime should be to dance freely for an hour to different music, stating that:

> "...gesture and dance are at the origin of music, and I certainly want
> to bring music back to that condition of ritual where everything
> you see is as important as what you hear, and not only the actions
> of producing sound, but also those creating the music-theatre"
> (Maconie, 1989: 145).

This notion ties in closely with original conceptions of the term *choreography*. Derived from the Greek *khoreia* (dance) and *graphein* (to write), *choreography* originally always intertwined dancing with singing, 'chorus' being "a dance in a circle, the persons singing and dancing, the chorus of a tragedy", from the Greek *khoros* meaning a "band of dancers or singers, dance or dancing ground" (Harper, 2012). It is therefore not surprising that in our approach and our interpretation of Stockhausen's *Tierkreis* we aimed to push the work also into a physical, body-oriented domain alongside considerations for employing dynamic subtleties and varying musical gestures.

This need for exploring a corporeal approach to contemporary music repertoire was influenced by our view that many contemporary music practices divorce the body from the musical statement that is being transmitted, with a particular reluctance on the part of musicians to engage in tactile relations with the other. Our physical exploration of performative bodies is not understood as a musical choreography but as a choreography that is shaped through the musical body itself. It is a modality that challenges existing methods of performance delivery, where traditionally the physical has been used only as a supplement to the communication of musical ideas, rather than as a creative focus. In our approach the music itself propelled forward choreographic ideas, the body becoming the driving force behind musical interpretation, while the physical articulation of space gave rise to different acoustic possibilities for melodic structure. Despite the fact that musicians develop what may be described as an intimate and tactile relationship with their instruments[2] – and a shared corporeal intimacy between bodies produced through playing together – there is currently little creative research explicitly addressing this concern.

This intimate relation inspired our creative decisions in reworking *Tierkreis* in which we explored the tactile relation between two performative bodies. We considered the relation between two players in terms of a "somatic interconnectedness" or "mutual tuning in relationship", which we believe critical to forming cohesive musical delivery (Schutz, 1951: 52 in Classen, 2005). Our physical relations in *Tierkreis* aimed at expressing this interconnectivity as an embodied process in which musical communication comes about through "felt coordinated movement" (Classen, 2005: 23). This conception ties in closely to the inter-relatedness of bodies within space as a kind of "umbilical continuity", in which the tactile relation between sounds and their source produce a centripetal dispersal within space (Connor, 2004b). We view the connection and coordination of our bodies on stage as facilitated through this sense of

---

2   Schroeder has argued elsewhere (2009: 150) that the physical relation between body and instrument must be understood as a quasi-incestuous relation – a relation of a performative body with her fetish object.

a common musical being in which sound provokes a desire for tactile relations between bodies, instruments and space.

Filippo Tommaso Marinetti, a member of the Futurist movement, was the first to propose an "educational scale of touch", suggesting that tactilism especially extends to "[...] young poets, pianists, stenographers, and to every erotic, refined, and powerful temperament" (Marinetti, 1921 in Classen, 2005: 331). Marinetti classifies six categories of touch, ranging from the "extremely confident, abstract and cold" to the "soft, hot, human" (Marinetti, 1921). Our explorations in *Tierkreis* identified a range of tactility in musical touch as well as touch between two performative bodies in such a way that qualities of physical movement and sound production were seen to be mutually dependent. Specifically, as performers of musical instruments, we were aware of a kind of visual sense, which, so Marinetti argues, is born in the fingertips. This learned tactilism in musicians – combined with an acute awareness that the physical sense inherent within music notation itself tends to be communicated much less – inspired us to question how musicians might rediscover such integral physicality.

Steven Connor, in his discussion of sound and touch, describes the skin as a "milieu of tactility" through which we form "sense-impressions" of the world around us, which in turn explore the "[...] border between self and non-self" (Connor, 2004a: 231). We used our explorations in *Tierkreis* as a platform to examine the threshold between self and other worked-through conceptions of tactility as a way into formulating a framework for a choreo-musical performance. Through this premise we investigated ways in which subjective experience interacts with bodily engagement as well as the dialogue between self and environment.

Drawing upon Susan Kozel's notion of performance as an ecosystem, we considered the inter-responsivity of performative aspects within *Tierkreis* as active elements feeding into a larger whole. These different elements are conceived of as a combination of "evolving parts" ("metabolisms") and "unanticipated responses" that are linked together through a network of relations that feed off and influence one another (Kozel, 2007: 207). In this way our performance recognises the self as an "[...] initiator of actions spreading outwards" that engages with otherness as part of a larger functionary system (*ibid*: 204). This approach emphasises the relation between things as interdependent, whereby distinctions occupying different boundaries may be used to explore bodily experience. This emphasis on the integration and convergence of various relations invites a methodology where meaning becomes polymorphous through a questioning of the "[...] capacity for affecting and being affected" (*ibid*: 206).

Kozel argues that in order to achieve optimum conditions for developing ecosystemic performance, an approach that balances fixed structural components with improvisatory elements may be adopted. In keeping with this conception, we developed a structure to our performance of *Tierkreis* that was neither wholly pre-scripted nor entirely random. We achieved this through developing a drawn score representing planned movements within the space which allowed room for differing approaches to elements such as the exact timing of bodily interaction during physical contact. We also used this framework to map out the shapes of specific signs of the zodiac over a stage layout template, as in Sagittarius and Pisces, to create an aerial dimension to our movement material reminiscent of constellations in the night sky. In this way, our two musical bodies were in constant expectation of things about to occur, ready to happen, leaving a space for a straining towards meanings. This state of being and intently listening allowed a certain state of self-reflection, in which, so Jean-Luc Nancy writes, the self becomes posited as a resonant subject (Nancy, 2007).

Our approach in reworking *Tierkreis* was influenced by principles established in contact improvisation, where physical attraction and resistance between one and the other suggests a kind of seductive playfulness. The flux of pressure and release between our two bodies engaged in musical delivery affected sound production in a variety of interesting ways. For example, in Gemini, the *pianissimo* touch of lighter passages where bodily resistance followed a physical ebbing away from the piano's keyboard was simultaneously matched by a physical pushing forwards and greater sonic force from the saxophone, where the body's movement compressed the diaphragm, thus increasing the volume of air projected through the instrument. The fact that the precise timings of this bodily interaction were unplanned not only allowed for variable physical delivery but also a flexibility in musical dynamics, tone quality, attack and articulation. The engagement of specific physical techniques in aiding and facilitating vocal projection is a well recognised branch of existing research, as with Tadashi Suzuki's method for actors (Suzuki, 1986). Through our interpretation of *Tierkreis*, we propose that this body knowledge, in which physical movement is used to support and influence sound production, may be successfully applied to the realms of instrumental playing in order to produce new modalities, leading to a framework for choreo-musical interpretations.

By engaging with Stockhausen's musical score in tandem with his ideas about an increased focus towards a physicality in musical delivery, our reworking of *Tierkreis* drew upon notions of tactility between two performative bodies. Employing notions of self and other informed by existing theoretical conceptions of touch, we have challenged traditional/historical models of musical performance in which physical contact between two players is considered taboo. We understand this physical relation to have an implicit erotic quality, since, as Chidester suggests, "...almost every tactile encounter may be invested with libidinous implications" (Chidester in Classen, 2005: 71). The seductive encounter implicitly inherent between two performative bodies engaged in physical contact introduces a playfulness to musical interpretation that carries a deeper inference for the inter-relation of the senses. The dependency of sound reception being reliant upon other senses, such as sight and touch (Connor, 2004b), and upon further senses, for instance proprioception and kinaesthesia (senses referring to motion and acceleration), equilibrioception (sense of balance as we explored in the sign of Taurus) and even nociception (sense of pain – as we explored in the signs of Gemini and Aries to some degree) is an invitation to propose a new methodology for music delivery that focuses on a body with those inter-related senses.

Our interpretation of Stockhausen relied upon this unity of sensation in which the flesh acts as the libidinous threshold where self and other mingle (Connor, 2004a) and where the performer "...sees and hears like she touches" (based on Levinas, 1989a: 79). In this way, our sense of corporeal interconnectedness – which has its roots in the sonic communication implicit within traditional performance models – becomes actualised by coming closer to touching the other's subjectivity. By exploring instrumental interactivity and bodily presence, guided by a choreo-musical approach to staff-notated repertoire that considers music beyond purely sonic terms, we explored the musical and physical relations implicit in the tactile engagement between body and instrument. This unification of musical and physical relations offers forth the tactility of interchange between instruments, musicians and space in order to bring the music back to a condition of ritual where "everything you see is as important as what you hear" (Stockhausen in Maconie, 1989: 145). It is in this sense that a choreographic approach to reinterpreting existing musical repertoire may offer an alternative to conventional models of music performance and that may lead to new and exciting interdisciplinary work.

Dr. Franziska Schroeder is a saxophonist and theorist, originally from Berlin. She received her PhD from the University of Edinburgh in 2006 for her research into performance and theories of embodiment. She has since written for many international journals, including *Leonardo*, *Organised Sound* and *Performance Research*. She has published a book on performance and the threshold and an edited volume on user-generated content for Cambridge Scholars. Forthcoming is an edited volume on Improvisation (2013). Franziska is a lecturer at the School of Creative Arts, Sonic Arts Research Centre at Queen's University Belfast, where she convenes modules in performance and critical theory.
f.schroeder@qub.ac.uk

Dr. Imogene Newland is a British researcher/practitioner specialising in interdisciplinary performance. Originally trained as a pianist, Imogene became interested in the intersection between choreographic practices and musical gesture in 2003. She has subsequently formed a series of practice-led works that address the intimate and intensely physical relationship between music and the body. In 2011 Imogene completed her practice-led PhD at the Sonic Arts Research Centre, Queen's University Belfast. She has presented her original performances at, amongst others, the Arnolfini, Bristol, the Klankkleur Festival, Amsterdam and Ars Electronica, Linz.
http://www.imogene-newland.co.uk/
imogene.newland@yahoo.com

Bibliography

Classen, C. (ed.) (2005) *The Book of Touch*, New York: Berg Publishers
Connor, S. (2004a) *The Book of Skin*, New York: Cornell University Press
Connor, S. (2004b) 'Edison's teeth: Touching hearing' in Erlmann, V. (ed.) *Hearing Cultures: Essays on Sound, Listening and Modernity*, New York: Berg Publishers

Deruchie, A. (2007) *Karlheinz Stockhausen: Tierkreis (Zodiac) (1974–75), (Karlheinz Stockhausen, arrangement)*. Programme-booklet for the North American première of "Fünf Sternzeichen", 5 March 2007. Montréal: Société de musique contemporaine du Québec

Kenyon, N. (1980*).* 'Musical Events: Seven Days' Wonder', *The New Yorker* (25 August): 78-81

Kozel, S. (2007) *Closer: Performance, Technologies, Phenomenology*, Cambridge, MA: MIT Press

Kurtz, M. (1992) *Stockhausen: A Biography* (trans. Toop, R.), London: Faber and Faber

Levinas, E. (1989a) 'Ethics as First Philosophy' in Hand, S. (ed.) *The Levinas Reader*, Oxford: Blackwell Publishers

Maconie, R. (1976) *The Works of Karlheinz Stockhausen*, London: Oxford University Press

Maconie, R. (ed.) (1989) *Stockhausen on Music: Lectures and Interviews*, London: Marion Boyars

Nancy, J-L. (2007) *Listening* (trans. Mandell, C.), New York: Fordham University Press

Schroeder, F. (2009) *Re-Situating Performance Within The Threshold: Performance practice understood through theories of embodiment*, Saarbrücken: VDM Verlag

Stockhausen, K.H (1975). *Tierkreis* (Werk Nr. 41 1/2), Kassel: Bärenreiter, 1988

Suzuki, T. (1986) *The Way of Acting: The theatre writings of Tadashi Suzuki* (trans. Rimer, J.T.), New York: Theatre Communications Group

URLs

Karlheinz Stockhausen - Official Website: www.stockhausen.org

Karlheinz Stockhausen Music Boxes - www.stockhausen.org/new_music_boxes.html

The Resilient Body

Developing Resilience and Presence Using the Feldenkrais Method

Campbell Edinborough

Abstract

This chapter presents an account of the resilient body: a body that is able to adapt to stress and recover from injury – attuned to the liveness of performance. The paradigm of the resilient body is framed through analysing the pedagogical approach used in the Feldenkrais Method.

Moshe Feldenkrais believed that the ability to adapt one's posture in order to feel comfortable in a range of situations and contexts was a vital part of developing potency as a human being. Through exploring Feldenkrais's ideas about human potency, and examining their connection with ideologies found within Judo, the author outlines the benefits of understanding the body as adaptive. He concludes by arguing that it is through recognising the adaptive capacity of the human body that the performer can develop resilience and potential, establishing a vital awareness of the constantly shifting movement of lived experience.

Jessica is lying on her back. She is examining how her ribs make contact with the floor. She begins to roll slowly from left to right, sensing the articulation of the different joints and muscles, noticing how she can keep her shoulder girdle quiet as her spine and rib cage move in relation to the floor. The movement of the ribs and spine is small to start with, but as she begins to learn how to differentiate the rib cage from the shoulder girdle, her range of movement grows. She rests, giving herself time to collect the different sensations in her awareness, before rolling onto her side to make her way up to sitting, and then slowly to standing.

Describing the feeling of standing, Jessica notes that she can feel the force of her body-weight being transmitted through her pelvis and hip joints, down her legs and into her heels. She says she feels taller and more grounded, but also lighter. She notes the increased space in her lower back and floating ribs, as well as the sensation of balance that comes from feeling her arms hanging from her shoulder girdle. She begins to walk, sensing the way in which the new alignment of her skeleton supports her weight in movement.

I ask her to stand still with her feet slightly wider than hip-width apart, inviting her to note the play of movement in her hips and spine, getting her to explore the 'small dance' of standing described by Steve Paxton (Paxton, 2009). I begin to press against Jessica's ribs with the palms of my hands, starting with a very small amount of pressure. I ask her to think about transferring the force from my hands down her spine, through her pelvis and legs into the floor.

As I increase the pressure, she begins to tense her abdomen and buttocks. I ask her to remain mindful of the amount of effort she is using to remain upright, encouraging her to focus on inhibiting the desire to push back or tense her muscles. I encourage her to think of the support of her skeleton, noting that she does not have to hold herself up. I feel her quality of effort change, she suddenly feels more solid and rooted.

The pressure I am transmitting into her ribcage has gradually increased. I am now pressing strongly, leaning into Jessica with a significant proportion of my weight. Despite the fact that I am much larger than her, she has managed to remain calm, sensing the support of her bones, inhibiting the reflexive desire to tense her muscles in response to my pushing. I slowly begin to release the pressure, bringing my hands away from her side. She takes a breath, mindfully expanding and contracting her chest before beginning to walk slowly around the space. She smiles, noting that she feels powerful yet also relaxed. She says, 'I feel calm, but ready to act.'

What is a resilient body? And what benefits might resilience have for the performer?

The quality of resilience refers to maintaining coherence and stability when under duress. It is impossible to train our muscles, skeleton and nervous system to transcend their material limitations; however, we can develop ways of keeping our balance when under physical and mental strain. In relative terms, humans are demonstrably weaker than most other mammals. Despite being larger, a human being is physically much less strong than a chimpanzee. The process of infancy in humans is extended far beyond that of our cousins in the animal kingdom, making us vulnerable and dependent on our social networks. However, as a species we have achieved unparalleled success in terms of our ability to reproduce and colonise different parts of the world. By harnessing our capacity to cope with novelty and change, humans have developed a unique, and somewhat paradoxical, kind of resilience – resilience based on the ability to respond and adapt to change.

Such resilience is of profound importance for performers, whose work demands the ability to reflect during action - consciously engaging with the performance as a living process (Edinborough, 2011). The liveness of theatre demands that when the performer walks on stage he actively responds to shifts in atmosphere, retaining enough balance to function effectively. Developing approaches for adapting to change has occupied a range of performance practitioners. Jacques Lecoq asked his students to examine the quality of neutrality, describing neutrality as a reference point for the actor – "a fulcrum that doesn't exist" (Lecoq, 2001: 36). Eugenio Barba described the state of pre-expressivity for the actor – a state of preparedness that exists before action or characterisation (Barba and Savarese, 1991: 219-234). In this chapter I am going to examine the way in which Moshe Feldenkrais aimed to forge resilience within the body and mind, making specific reference to his engagement with the martial arts (particularly Judo), and reflecting on some of the ways in which the forms of resilience that he described might benefit individuals engaged in live performance.

Moshe Feldenkrais sought to question what terms such as 'resilience' and 'potency' might mean when related to human experience. He investigated how it might be possible to remain balanced when engaged in the constant process of movement dictated by life. Feldenkrais recognised that life presents us with a constant stream of novelty and the unknown. Through recognising this fact, he intuited that human resilience stemmed not from our material strength, but from our ability to learn and recover.

"...life is not a stable process. Stability is for trees. For us, life is a process of risk and recovery. Each step we take is a risk. The ability to recover is our greatest quality." (Feldenkrais in Fox, 1979).

In order to function, both as performers and as individuals, we need to maintain physical and mental stability, yet we must also continually adapt to the constant process of movement we encounter in our environment. We can train our muscles to be more powerful and, to a certain extent, develop the material resilience of our bones; however, such training is meaningless if we have not learned to differentiate between intelligent and unintelligent action. A performer does not necessarily need significant strength or great flexibility. However, he does need to be aware of the constant process of movement and change within his experience. He needs to develop the potential to adapt to the ever-changing circumstances of the live event.

Feldenkrais's complex understanding of human functioning was influenced by his study of neurology, cybernetics and the emerging somatic practices of his time. It was, however, his experience of the Japanese martial art of Judo that defined the way that he related the cultivation of awareness to the development of human potency and resilience. Although there is little reference to Judo within Feldenkrais's books about his Method, his books about Judo (Feldenkrais, 1951; 2010), and interviews with those interested in the relationship between martial arts and the Feldenkrais Method (Leri, 2010; Segal, 1995), suggest the many ways in which the practice of Judo informed the development of his thinking.

As a form of self-defence, Judo places practitioners in a highly specific situation. In order to defend himself, the Judo practitioner is required to solve tactical puzzles, demanding the maintenance of mental and emotional calm. He is required to maintain stability (in the broadest sense) when under attack, sustaining physical and mental balance as the attacker attempts to throw him or pin him to the floor. The fact that the attacker's movement and balance is also constantly changing demands that the practitioner remain supple and mindful during the process of defence. The Judo practitioner must recognise that nothing is fixed within the interaction between attacker and defender.

Judo creates a competitive situation in which an individual's resilience and potential are constantly tested. In the book, *Higher Judo: Groundwork*,

Feldenkrais highlighted the importance of not relying on pre-formed solutions to problems, stating that the Judo practitioner must be able to change his mind when engaged in the process of defence and attack (2010: 94). He noted that Jigaro Kano, the founder of Judo, had a tremendous ability to regain his balance and evade attacks (Leri, 2010: 148), claiming that success in Judo competition was rooted in the process of trying to recover equilibrium faster than one's opponent (*ibid*: 154).

Feldenkrais would later profess to teach the Feldenkrais Method in exactly the same way that he taught Judo (*ibid*: 149). Within both practices, movement patterns are practised and repeated, with the student or practitioner focusing on "detecting small differences" (Feldenkrais, 1984: 15), developing an ever clearer sense of optionality within movement in order to find ways to recover one's balance and move with greater ease.

Jessica stands with her feet hip-width apart and again notes the play of movement in her body. I ask her to sense the freedom in her shoulders, encouraging her to notice the way that her spine balances over her pelvis, supported by her legs. Asking her to keep a mindful connection to her physical sensation, I begin to push against her shoulders, chest and back. This time, instead of standing still and redirecting the force through her skeleton and into the ground, Jessica's task is to move in such a way as to draw me off balance.

She waits to feel the direction of my push before transferring her weight to the left or right foot, turning her hips, and moving me by redirecting the force I am providing. As the speed of the game increases, tension starts to appear in her shoulders. She is trying to pre-empt my movement and ends up fighting against me. I remind her not to overstretch herself, suggesting that she feels her connection to the floor through her feet, encouraging her to wait to feel the pressure I am providing. She focuses on maintaining her own balance as she moves, keeping a softness within her movements, guided by mindful awareness of her relationship to gravity.

I begin to increase the speed and force of my pushing, changing direction more frequently. Jessica maintains her calm. She keeps redirecting my movement, opening her hip joints, softening her shoulders and arms, breathing into her lower abdomen and activating her pelvic floor so that she can move her legs without losing balance. She guides me around the room, as if we are dancing,

differentiating the subtle shifts in pressure of my pushing by maintaining her
awareness of the present moment.

It is common to think of martial arts as practices relating only to combat;
however, arts like Judo provide us with opportunities to study the way that
we respond to losing our balance. Feldenkrais recognised how the practice
of attending mindfully to the way in which one responds to physical and
mental pressure enables one to develop the skill of resilience. Through
refining this process in his own method, he found ways to utilise the human
nervous system's flexibility and aptitude for adaptation in order to combat
challenging situations, creating a specific and complex paradigm of strength
and intelligence.

Feldenkrais argued that our experience of movement shapes the way
that we think and feel, and vice versa (1990: 30-39). Taking this belief
to its logical conclusion, he worked on the assumption that anxiety and
trauma were connected to patterns of muscular excitation in the nervous
system (2005: 114). He noted that loss of balance, or any action performed
without awareness, is accompanied by the undifferentiated excitement of
neurons in the motor cortex (2002: 85). When someone trips or falls, it
is common for him to tense his muscles. This tensing of the muscles in the
body is a protective mechanism; however, such muscular activity does not
necessarily represent the most intelligent form of functioning. Part of the
process of developing human resilience depends, therefore, on learning how
to coordinate our responses to stimuli within the environment.

> "Learning to inhibit unwanted contractions of muscles that
> function without, or in spite of, our will, is the main task of
> coordinating action. We have to learn to inhibit those cells of the
> motor cortex to which the excitation spreads. Before we become
> able to excite a precise pattern of cells in the wanted order, the
> neighbouring cells all along the pattern of the cells essential to the
> movement become active. After adequate apprenticeship, when
> proficiency is achieved, only cells that command the muscles for
> the desired performance alone send out impulses. All the others
> are inhibited. Without this inhibition, no coordinated action is
> possible." (*ibid*: 85)

In order to overcome the anxiety associated with a stimulus such as tripping or falling, the individual has to be able to differentiate between functional muscular activity and non-functional, parasitic muscular activity. Feldenkrais claimed that: "The experience of difficulty or resistance to action is indirectly due to imperfect inhibition of the cells commanding the antagonists of muscles that are indispensable in forming the desired pattern" (*ibid*: 85). It is anxiety, and the subsequent failure to differentiate between proper and improper action, that creates resistance and discomfort, not the activity of work itself.

As I noted earlier, I am considerably larger than Jessica. However, by harnessing her awareness so as to mindfully differentiate between functional and non-functional action, she was able to coordinate her movement to redirect the force I was transmitting into her body. Through studying her self-image during the processes of rolling and standing, Jessica developed enough awareness of the subtle articulations between her ribs, spine and pelvis to enable her to maintain her balance while under duress. Instead of contracting the muscles in her abdomen and legs in order to fight the pressure being transmitted into her torso, she focused on maintaining her posture. She let the functional integrity of her skeleton support both her weight and mine.

The innate flexibility of the human nervous system enables individuals to overcome challenges encountered in the environment; however, the ability to harness this flexibility during action requires cultivation. When I first began to push Jessica she became anxious about falling over. She tensed her muscles, trying to fight the force I was transmitting into her torso. The use of such effort dictated a loss of awareness of the subtle variations within the direction and strength of the forces being transmitted into her body. It was only when she was encouraged not to rely on a pre-prepared pattern of muscular action that she was able to regain her balance. She needed to actively attend to the movements taking place in her body and in mine in order to differentiate between intelligent, functional action and unintelligent, compulsive action. She needed to find her balance – become alive to movement as a process.

While Jessica's case study demonstrates a pragmatic, physical manifestation of pressure and stress, it strikes me that the stress associated with being pushed is not so different from the pressure to perform in a live event. In terms of the performer's experience, the weight of a firm push is not terribly dissimilar to the weight of expectation created by the interaction between performer and spectator. A challenge is made to the performer and there is no guarantee of success. Just as in Jessica's lesson, the process of performance demands that the performer establish a sense of comfort without losing functionality in action. Intelligence in the context of live performance demands walking a fine line between action and reflection.

In order to cultivate the kind of embodied, mindful awareness demonstrated by Jessica's lessons, the Feldenkrais Method invites students to compare subtle differences in their experience of movement. One of Feldenkrais's 'AWARENESS THROUGH MOVEMENT' lessons might begin with the teacher asking the student to compare the experiential differences between the way his left foot and his right foot make contact with the floor. This examination might then continue up the length of the body, with the student assessing the differences between the legs, the two sides of the pelvis, the shoulders and arms.

Feldenkrais made it clear that the student should not alter his position when attending to such qualitative differences; nor should the student judge differences as good or bad. The Feldenkrais Method asserts that it is only through developing a mindful, non-judgemental attitude towards the self-image that learning, and thus resilience, can be achieved. Feldenkrais often noted that a change in the habitual pattern of how the body moves feels like an error when assessed with reference to our habitual self-image. In a Feldenkrais lesson, the student is encouraged not to be seduced by the need to achieve a specific goal, such as touching the toes, or going into the splits. Feldenkrais teachers dissuade students from attempting to push beyond their comfortable capacities because the Method recognises that over-stretching in order to fulfil a task only serves to reinforce existing habits.

Despite the fact that he was interested in promoting human resilience and potency, Feldenkrais understood that in order to develop new patterns of action, the individual must remain in a state of comfort and ease, where the movements being explored do not invoke self-protecting reflexes. To truly explore a movement, the student must disregard pre-existing notions of what such a movement should feel like; he must be able to experience it without making a judgement about whether the experience is right or wrong. Only then can the student truly experience the movement without reference to his preconceptions, and only then can he allow the movement to provide information enabling him to surpass his limitations.

The Feldenkrais Trainer Carl Ginsburg explained this to me in physiological terms during my own Feldenkrais Practitioner Training. Ginsburg noted that whenever a muscle is overstretched (forced beyond its comfortable limits) the stretch reflex is invoked in order to protect the muscle from tearing. The stretch reflex contracts the muscles being stretched. This process denies the possibility for such a movement to create change in the neuromuscular patterning of the student, because the invoked contraction will be carried out in relation to pre-existing patterning. Stretching invokes a pre-existing model of the self-image, disallowing the possibility for growth and change.

Ginsburg's example serves, in a material and pragmatic way, to demonstrate that Feldenkrais did not introduce mindful engagement with self-experience as an end in itself. Awareness is a means for developing the ability to grow and recover – a means to establish resilient and intelligent functioning. For Feldenkrais, the ability to differentiate mindfully marked an ability to develop new courses of action.

One of the fundamental reasons for utilising such a complex approach to learning new movements, and curbing the impulse to achieve instant results, stems from the fact that human beings are non-trivial systems. In a trivial system, such as an automobile, one can predict the outcome in relation to the input. In a non-trivial system this is not the case. In a system as complex as a human being, it is impossible to predict what kind of output will be created in relation to a specific input.

The human nervous system contains countless neural connections and feedback systems that affect, and are affected by, the process of responding to stimuli. If we ask two people to follow a series of simple instructions, their individual responses will contain many differences. Although both the stimulus and the structure of the muscular-skeletal systems could be the same in the two people, the nervous system in each individual will have a variety of different patterns, which will, in turn, affect the nature of their responses to stimuli. Even if we were able to map the billions of connections that pattern actions in the self, it would still be extremely difficult to predict the outcome of an input in a person, because the nervous system is living, and thus constantly changing in relation to new stimuli and to the feedback shaped by existing patterns in the self-image.

If the student (or teacher) already has a picture of what the process of change should feel like, the process will be judged with explicit reference to the pre-existing patterns of self that define the individual's experience. This defies the nature of change and development. Although the student must enter into a process of comparing the effects of change, it is imperative that he does not compare the changes in relation to a detailed, pre-formed expectation. Such expectation can only serve to validate and enforce existing patterns within the self-image, or create frustration in the student. The resilient ability to recover requires openness to difference and complexity.

In the case study I presented scenarios in which a student was placed under considerable physical pressure. In each lesson, Jessica started to respond to the pressure of my pushing by indiscriminately tensing her muscles. However, with some direction, she began to focus less on the pressure I was creating and more on the process of maintaining her own balance – feeling the support of her skeleton and the small variations of movement at the point of contact between my hands and her ribcage. Jessica's experience serves to demonstrate the value of mindfully attending to variations in physical experience in order to maintain balance. Her example shows that the resilience of the human body is not found in the material strength of our muscles and bones, but in the ability to bring awareness to the constantly shifting nature of our experience.

Although the performer's body is often referred to as an instrument, the paradigm that Feldenkrais's work presents frames this description as a reductive misconception. The performer cannot shape his body to repeat the same action again and again for an audience. The performer's body is the fabric of his experience, his connection to the environment and to other people. To fail to recognise the body as a process is to lose contact with the present moment that drives and shapes performance.

To stand on stage in performance, or in rehearsal, demands an active commitment to the present moment. The mindful resilience promoted within the Feldenkrais Method demonstrates that the performer can understand his presence not as a quality, but as an activity. Through connecting mindfully with the subtleties of his embodied experience, the performer can develop the ability to recover and find balance. He can find strategies to reflect and discriminate during the process of action. In an art form so dependent on the quality of live interaction, Feldenkrais's account of human resilience seems to be invaluable. His conception of resilience provides the performer with an opportunity to overcome the stress and anxiety of live performance by encouraging us to harness the benefits of our evolutionary inheritance.

Dr. Campbell Edinborough is a Lecturer in Drama and Theatre Practice at the University of Hull. His research applies somatic paradigms of experience and cognition to the study of dance, theatre and performance. This research is informed by his study of somatic practices and his work as a Feldenkrais practitioner and theatre maker. He has published and presented papers on performance training, somatics, and performance and cognition. His current research is interested in the study of liminal spaces as sites for empathetic engagement and deliberation.
a.edinborough@hull.ac.uk

Bibliography

Barba, E. and Savarese, N. (1991) *The Dictionary of Theatre Anthropology: The Secret Art of the Performer*, London: Routledge

Edinborough, C. (2011) 'Developing decision-making skills for performance through the practice of mindfulness in somatic training', *Theatre, Dance and Performance Training* 2.1, pp.18-33.

Feldenkrais, M. (1951) *Judo: The Art of Defence and Attack,* London: Frederick Warne

_____ (1984) *The Master Moves*, ed. Carl Ginsburg. Capitola, CA: Meta

_____ (1990) *Awareness Through Movement,* London: Penguin Arkana

_____ (2002) *The Potent Self: A guide to spontaneity*, Berkeley, CA: North Atlantic Books

_____ (2005) *Body and Mature Behaviour,* Berkeley, CA: North Atlantic Books

_____ (2010) *Higher Judo: Groundwork,* Berkeley, CA: North Atlantic Books

Fox, C. (1979) 'The Feldenkrais Phenomenon.' *Quest*, No. 7, Dec./Jan. Available at www.bit.ly/TPbody03

Hanna, T. (1995) 'Interview with Mia Segal' in Johnson, D. H. (ed.) *Bone, Breath and Gesture: Practices of Embodiment*, Berkeley, CA: North Atlantic Books

Lecoq, J. (2001) *The Moving Body: Teaching Creative Theatre*, (trans. Bradby, D.), London: Methuen

Leri, D. (2010) 'The Extraordinary Story of How Moshe Feldenkrais Came to Study Judo' in Beringer, E. (ed.) *Embodied Wisdom: The Collected Papers of Moshe Feldenkrais*. Berkeley, CA: North Atlantic Books

Paxton, S. (2009) 'Steve Paxton's Talk at CI36 – Excerpts.' *Contact Quarterly*, Vol. 34 No. 1, Winter/Spring. Available at www.bit.ly/TPbody04

The Imaginal Body

Using Imagery and the Principles of the Alexander Technique to Release the Imagination

Niamh Dowling

Abstract

This lens, this way of seeing through the body, begins by identifying habitual patterns, using conscious thinking, anatomical images and visualisations. The hypothetical case study with an actress (Kate) focuses in the first instance on setting up the conditions to release restrictive patterns of physical use, with an underpinning of the Alexander Technique. For the purposes of this lens, an important distinction is articulated between visualising and imagining and clarifying notions of imagination and memory. The case study culminates in revealing the imaginative content of the text.

Kate is an actress who is playing the character of Maurya in Riders to the Sea *by J.M.Synge. She says she feels blocked imaginatively and wants to do some work on her arms which she experiences as being 'disconnected' from the rest of her body. I observe that she has tension in her shoulders and neck and that her spine, rib cage and diaphragm are compressed. She is pulling her head back and down, shortening the muscles of her neck, which causes her to push her chin forward, collapse in the front of her body, tighten in her rhomboids and misuse the external muscles of her back.*

Through the stiffening of her neck and pulling back of her head, Kate triggers a series of habitual muscular responses that restrict her movement and produce a compression in her spine and the misuse of her whole body and voice. This causes a change in her musculature and posture, in the shape of her diaphragm and in her breathing, constriction in the throat and neck and a change in her body's relationship to gravity. In performance this pattern will become exaggerated, putting pressure on Kate's vocal folds and creating more tension in her neck, shoulders and arms. The way she consciously or unconsciously does things in her everyday life affects the way she functions, and therefore the way she performs.

F.M. Alexander (1869-1955), creator of the Alexander Technique, also had a tendency to pull his head back and tighten the back of his neck. Alexander tried to stop himself doing this by correcting the position of his head, and over-stretching the muscles in his neck. He realised that 'doing' something had not rectified the problem so he began to concentrate on thinking rather than doing. He thought specifically that he wanted his head to go forward and up and that he didn't want it to go back and down. By inhibiting or stopping a habitual response and thinking in action Alexander set in motion the muscular mechanism essential to good physical use. This helped him to stay in the present and not to end-gain – or to rush to create a 'correct' postural position.

End-gaining produces tension in trying to reach the goal without much thought as to how to get there. When the process takes priority over the result, the muscles are instead being taught how to stay in the present, how to move from moment to moment, from thought to thought and not to jump to a result. In another article (Dowling, 2008) I applied this principle to the actor, who by not anticipating what she knows will happen in the scene, allows it to play out and to reveal the outcome gradually. Staying in the moment is an essential aspect of an actor's process for both rehearsal and performance. That process begins in this work with Kate at a deep, muscular and sensory level through specific conscious thinking and subsequently is developed through visualisation to release the imagination.

We look at anatomical pictures of the muscles of the back, the trapezii and the latissimi dorsi whose function is related to the movement of the arms and connecting the arms into the back. I then trace these muscles on Kate's back from the base of the skull and spine out to her arms and shoulders to position for her the insertion and origin of the muscles and to give her an experiential embodiment of the two muscles. This experiential anatomy helps in identifying for Kate the way in which she is tightening and shortening her back and neck muscles and how the misuse of the muscles of her neck at the origin of the trapezius is creating tension in her shoulders and arms.

The underlying principles of the work with Kate are rooted in the Alexander Technique, which offers a particular approach to performer training. At the centre of an actor' s training is a search for a way to respond truthfully in the moment to imagined circumstances. Stress and nerves can exaggerate an everyday pattern of use, resulting in physical and vocal misuse, over-contracted muscles and an unbalanced skeletal system. As a result, body and voice become tight, actions and lines are anticipated, rhythms become erratic, emotional responses are demonstrated and the audience cannot hear, see or receive the images inherent in the text.

Having established an anatomical picture as a starting point, Kate lies on her back on the floor in semi-supine, with knees bent and feet resting on the floor. Semi-supine is an excellent way to start changing the process of deterioration and compression in the spine. Bending the knees allows the curve of the lower back to open out and extend and the neck to gently stretch. I ask Kate to picture her spine in her body, positioning it in its actual place. I guide her verbally through visualising each vertebra on the floor and the discs between each vertebra filling up with body fluid. The discs expand like small sponges soaking up liquid. As each disc expands, it pushes the vertebrae on either side away from the disc and there is a knock-on lengthening effect through the spine in two directions, towards the head and towards the pelvis. Kate is visualising, or picturing this process, rather than 'doing' something obviously physical. Taking the weight of her head in my hands, I guide her verbally through the specifics of the Alexander directions, which give detailed 'directions' or instructions to the nervous system: to allow the neck to be free and to direct the head forward and up in such a way that the back lengthens and widens, widening across the upper part of the arms and the knees releasing forward and up.

This lens, this way of seeing through the body, begins by exploring anatomical pictures, specific and conscious thinking, images and visualisations and the impact these are having in releasing habitual restrictive patterns of use. It is helpful at this point to understand neuroscientist Antonio Damasio's (1994) model of 'the body-minded brain' as a finely balanced synthesis between mind, brain, body and environment, where the whole organism generates responses to and from the environment and itself, rather than the conventional notion of 'image' as a visual picture at the forefront of consciousness. Damasio's model is succinctly summarised by performance-maker and researcher Kate Hunter (2012) in identifying how the brain processes this reactive and generative information and connectivity by forming neuronal disposition we know as thought. The brain forms images in response to immediate external stimuli but also recalls images from the past. Hunter continues this summary of Damasio's model (the italics are mine):

> "An 'image' can be a feeling, a sound, a bodily experience, a recollection, a thought, a fragment of past experience, a touch. Images are *perceptual* (informed by senses or experiences in the present moment) or *recalled* (informed by previous recollections). Images are not located in or formed by the brain alone—the brain, the body and the environment are fully involved in the generation of an image." (Hunter, 2012)

Coming back to actress Kate in semi supine position, she is in a state of active relaxation and her brain is working at the level of perceptual images as articulated by Damasio. Active relaxation involves a high level of awareness aiming to consciously reduce levels of tension and stress. Having studied anatomical pictures, Kate visualises or has a mental picture or image of the anatomical information *in situ*, in her body in its actual place. In visualising she forms an image of something that is invisible and makes it visible. Kate is making the invisible spine visible to herself so that she can change or transform it with her thoughts and images. She visualises the muscles of the back *in situ* in order to be precise about their position in her body.

It is important to also notice the role that touch plays as another simultaneous input in receiving and processing sensory information. The use of touch by teachers of the Alexander Technique is very specific in its intent and character and uses feedback from three modes; visual, tactile and proprioceptive. The teacher uses their hands to demonstrate directly a quality of easy and unforced movement that brings the student's attention to areas that may be habitually out of the student's awareness. While at times a teacher's touch may vary as required by the particulars of the moment, it is at all times educational and non-invasive. Kate is guided and assisted by light, guiding touch in the head-neck area. This touch facilitates the neuromuscular response of spinal lengthening, allowing Kate to experience the sensation of release and direction and lengthening in her spine.

Kate remains in semi supine while I move and lengthen each arm out from her spine in order for her to experience the trapezius and latissimus connecting her arms into her back, widening across her back and the upper part of her arms. As I move her arms I ask her to picture the two muscles jointly forming the image of wings, wide expansive wings attaching to each vertebrae of her spine. Coming to stand, Kate begins to move her imaginary wings, extending the image down to her legs and feet so the image is embodied through all of her body, her movement and the imagined environment. I have chosen to work on the arms as it is a specific tension pattern identified by Kate and the image of the back muscles as wings offers an example of a clear developmental journey from anatomy through visualisation to movement. The imagined activity of flying encourages Kate to move freely maintaining the Alexander directions and anatomical connections that have been set up.

For the purposes of this lens, I make an important distinction between visualising and imagining. In this context I use visualisation to capture the essence of positioning and placing the image inside the body, in order to create an accurate sensory picturing or mapping of Kate's structure. Imagining herself flying on the other hand will stimulate this visualisation to come alive in the body and mind, so Kate imagines that she is flying. These images or constructions of the brain are explained by Damasio (1994):

> "It appears they are concocted by a complex neural machinery of perception, memory and reasoning. Sometimes the construction is paced from the world outside the brain, that is, from the world inside our body or around it, with a bit of help from past memory. Sometimes the construction is directed entirely from within our brain, by our sweet and silent thought process, from the top down, as it were. That is the case, for instance, when we recall a favourite melody, or recall visual scenes with our eyes closed and covered, whether the scenes are a replaying of a real event or an imagined one."

The philosopher Alan Ross White discusses the relationship between the notion of imagining, imagination and other concepts like supposing, believing and pretending. He concludes his discussion by defining imagination as the mental construction of a possibility. He states that to imagine is to think of something as possibly being so. Imagination is linked to discovery, invention and originality because it is a thought of the possibility rather than of the actual reality of what might or could be. The imagination is not a separate faculty. It is what happens when the faculties we all have are freed from their usual limitations and restrictions.

I ask Kate to open her arms and to imagine herself in flight and I guide her verbally on an imaginary flight that takes her travelling over lands and seas, deserts and villages, roads, fields and cities. She moves with ease and freedom in our studio and in her mind on the flight, flying, swirling, diving, swooping and coming to rest on top of a mountain. She imagines she feels the earth below her feet and sky above her head and the river valley in front of her, the sounds, the colours and the wide open space around her. As she stands on the peak of the mountain, I gently put my hands on her head and neck. I feel the crown of her head lengthen up towards the sky and the soles of her feet go down towards the earth and in between her spine is lengthening. I notice how her chest expands and her shoulders fall into her back. Her body is connected, she is strong and powerful, she is grounded and directed. She speaks her text - discovering what lies within the text while imposing nothing on it. The images in the text become alive and inner thoughts and feelings of the character are revealed.

Having committed to the imaginary circumstances, Kate starts a flow of consciousness. One thought follows another and one image stimulates the next image. The phenomenon of how one idea may call up another in consciousness was first set out in the Law of Contiguity, one of Aristotle's Laws of Association, as defined by psychologist George Boeree (2000):

> "Things or events that occur close to each other in space or time tend to get linked together in the mind."

It was Thomas Hobbes however, who linked this contiguity to the imaginative process. He argued that:

> "the power of the mind to relate similar images to one another is augmented by the mental habit of contiguous association: the

ability of one image to recall another that has previously been connected with it" (Brett, 1969: 15).

For example, imagining flying and arriving on the top of the mountain stimulates associations and images of rivers, sky, birds and even feelings and sounds. Hobbes breaks ground in the psychological description he gives of the mental processes involved in imaginative composition when he argues that imagination is fundamentally a form of memory; a memory freed to some degree from the restrictions of actual experience.

Most people assume that when a significant event occurs to us, we somehow place the record of such an event in some kind of neural filing system – a huge storage drive that acts as a repository for everything that has ever happened in our lives, everybody we have ever met, every flower we ever have smelled. At some later time, when we want to recall the memory, the brain accesses the drive, searches through the many files of events and stories, and selects the memory for us to peruse. It appears in our consciousness, seemingly unchanged, the facts clearly evident, exactly as it occurred, sometimes in incredibly specific detail. The brain files all our memorial information in this way, allowing us to find what we need relatively easily and bring it to consciousness. We believe this to be true because our experience tells us so – we remember things exactly as they happened. Or do we?

Damasio argues that in fact images are not stored as pictures, feelings, things or events and that there is direct evidence that whenever we recall an object or event we do not get a precise and exact reproduction but rather an interpretation:

> "Recalled images tend to be held in consciousness only fleetingly and although they may appear to be good replicas, they are often inaccurate and incomplete" (Damasio, 1994: 101)

Furthermore Damasio explains that:

> "The images we reconstitute in recall occur side by side with the images formed upon stimulation from the exterior. The images reconstituted from the brain's interior are less vivid than those promoted by the exterior." (*ibid*: 115)

Working with images can be a very powerful teaching tool. We can make a mental request through imagery which can be more effective than a strong verbal instruction as the image works indirectly to accomplish technical tasks and remove tensions.

Kate writes of her experience in the exercise:

'Letting go the tension in my shoulders liberated me. The image of the muscles which became wings and imagining myself flying helped me to connect to the energetic life of my body and to allow it to dance – in a way I was the bird and I danced with the bird and the bird I danced with was my own impulse to move and discover. It felt like a natural flow of energy and impulses as I didn't have to think about where to go or how to move but instead just let my body and my imagination take me on its journey. I didn't feel as though I was in a trance because my body was leading me, I felt the opposite, I felt physically connected and alive, as though I could sustain this exploration for ages. I could taste my freedom. When I stopped, I experienced the surrounding space as being clearer, charged with energy and brighter to my senses. By being in the flow of my imagination I felt open to the energy of other people around me, I let them in and they became part of my world in the here and now. When I spoke I heard myself differently. I don't think I have ever really heard my voice before. I spoke Maurya's lines:

"They are all gone now and there isn't anything more the Sea can do to me... I'll have no call now to be up crying and praying when the wind breaks from the south, and you can hear the surf is in the east, and the surf is in the west, making a great stir with the two noises. I'll have no call to be going down and getting Holy Water in the dark nights after Samhain and I won't care what way the sea is when the other woman will be keening."

I am sure I experienced myself for a brief time as the woman in my text and the voice of the woman was speaking through me. Furthermore I was touched by the sorrow and pain of loss within the text. Tears were running down my cheeks as I spoke. The text touches the loss of the woman, my own imagined and real memories and experience of loss, and our individual and collective loss of loved ones, of love, of hope, of future, of nations, of culture, of youth, of time, of freedom, all mingled with my own joy at finding my voice.'

Kate describes the experience as transformative, not only at a physical and personal level, but also in relation to the subsequent performance of the loss within the text and her interpretation of the character of Maurya. She reveals the grieving woman in her isolation talking about the storm and the crashing waves, the sound of the wind mingled with the sound of the women keening for the drowned man and the end of harvest and the beginning of the darker, winter of her life. She captures the rhythm of the language and the poetic dialogue of rural Ireland, pain, loss, loneliness, the lack of purpose, the hopelessness and the grief. She also reveals aspects of the lifestyle, rituals, history, geography, landscape, religion, tides, hardship, isolation and the hopeless struggle of a people against the relentless power of the sea.

Kate captures many of the complexities of the process of imagination in her writing about the experience of the imaginary flight; both perceptual images and recalled images are present, feelings and physical sensations, spatial awareness, memories and interpretations. These stimulate and inform a deep connection to the text and are a reminder that the process of imagination is much more than originality and new discoveries and how it can co-articulate the known and the unknown, the visible and the invisible. The development of the imagination is a vital element of the actor's training. Moreover it is also a vital element of how we express every moment of our lives, how experiences resonate in us and are infused with feelings and memories and fears and possibility. It is an everyday thing as well as a magical thing and is the source of great joy, fulfilment, creativity and endless potential.

Niamh Dowling is Head of School of Performance at Rose Bruford College of Theatre and Performance in London. She has worked extensively internationally as a Movement Director, leading workshops in the UK, Europe, USA, Asia, South and Central America and Russia. Niamh trained as a teacher of The Alexander Technique and in movement with Monika Pagneux in Paris and Ann Bogart, Nancy Topf and Eva Karczag in New York. She has collaborated closely with Teatr Piesn Kozla in Poland for the past ten years. Niamh has a holistic approach to education and performance training with emphasis on interconnectedness of movement and voice and is one of the practitioners on the recently launched online Routledge Performance Archive.
niamh.dowling@bruford.ac.uk

Bibliography

Alexander, F.M. (1985) *Use of the Self,* London: Methuen

Andrews, M. and Barter, S. (2002) *The Alexander Technique and the Actor* www.alexandertechnique.com/articles/acting/

Boeree, G. (2000) *Psychology: The Beginning,* www.bit.ly/TPbody02

Brett, R. L. (1969) *Fancy and Imagination,* London: Methuen

Damasio, A. (1994) *Descartes' Error: Emotion, Reason and The Human Brain*, New York: Penguin

Dowling, N. (2012) *Alexander Technique into Performance*, Routledge Performance Archive. Available at www.digitaltheatre.com/routledge

_____ (2011) 'Teatr Piesn Kozla training and its integration into Western European theatre training' in *Theatre Dance and Performance Training*, Vol. 2, 2

_____ (2008/2011) *Moving into Performance: Using the Principles Of the Alexander Technique to Underpin and Enhance An Actor's Training.* Available at www.bit.ly/TPbody01

Harpur, P. (2002) *The Philosopher's Secret Fire: A History of the Imagination*, Southport: The Squeeze Press

Heirich, Jane R. (2005) *Voice and the Alexander Technique,* San Francisco, CA: Mornum Time Press

Hunter, K. (2012) 'Facts and Fictions: Landscapes of Memory, Imagination and The Brain in Performance-Making' in *Compass Points: The Locations, Landscapes and Coordinates of Identities in Contemporary Performance Making*, Australasian Association for Drama Theatre and Performance Studies (ADSA), Brisbane: Queensland University of Technology

Kurjata, P. (2012) MA Acting Journal, Manchester Metropolitan University

Park, G. (2005) *The Art of Changing: Exploring the Alexander Technique and Its Relationship with The Human Energy Body,* Bath: Ashgrove Publishing

Synge, John Millington (1904) *Riders to the Sea*, A Public Domain Book

White, A. R. (1990) *The Language of the Imagination*, Oxford: Basil Blackwell

The Learnt Body

The Body as a Reflection of Socio-Cultural Responses to Landscape[1]

Nicholas Hope

Abstract

Based on a participant-observation research project with theatre companies in Oslo, Norway and Sydney, Australia, the author suggests that the learnt body incorporates a physicality and sense of proximal space that is in part defined by the historic, socio-cultural responses of the prevailing community to the meta-geographic and lived urban landscape that the body inhabits.

The chapter draws on the work of Maurice Merleau-Ponty, Edward Casey, Jaana Parviainen and RUDOLF LABAN amongst others to help give shape to the relatively detailed and intensive notes and interviews undertaken during the placement, as well as referring to the author's experience as an actor, performer and resident in both places. Laban's terminology is used to describe movement and body-weight use during the observed rehearsals.[2]

The work and the resulting discussion lead the author to propose that one way to approach the training of the body is to first investigate and isolate the socio-culturally learnt aspects of its place-memory: to familiarise the self with what is based in learnt body memory in order to consciously transcend socially coded habits and movement patterns.

---

1   Some of the core material in this chapter has been previously published in my article 'Embodied Landscape: the place of geography in the actor's creation of character' (Hope, 2011) in the service of a different discussion.

2   For a summary of Laban notation, see the Glossary and Adrian (2002).

The body out-of-place

Winter, Oslo, 1996: As an Australian Sydney-sider walking outside at the peak of winter I was advised to keep the area of the mouth and nose warm and to be aware of the effects of breathing sub-zero air into moisture-lined mouth and nostrils. I had to re-learn how to walk to avoid slipping and falling; this included using heavier footwear, thereby changing the speed and angle of my pacing. I had to attempt to realign how I transferred weight from foot to foot, including how I placed my feet on the ground: weight needed to be transferred in a more vertical alignment than I was used to. I was taught this by a Norwegian co-actor on a film made in the countryside in winter: I needed to look like I was used to being there, not "like a tourist", as the director said.[3] My physical presence became more marked, overt: my body was foreign to this place, and became focally present to me in a way it was not in the already embodied physicality of my-body-in-the-geographic/climatic-familiarity of Sydney. These physical changes alone affected my sense of well-being and equilibrium, and underlined some of the basic formative differences existing between myself and those I worked with in terms of socio-culturally inherited, day-to-day bodily skills.
(Hope, 2010)

In 2007, after many years working as an actor around the world, I undertook a comparative analysis of two sets of theatre rehearsals in, respectively, Oslo and Sydney, and considered the results in terms of 'self' and 'place' as inter-animating concepts. The results confirmed my own experience, uncovering a set of ubiquitous differences between each cast that appeared to reflect a socio-cultural response to their lived environments. Whilst it was impossible to verify, I concluded that the learnt body incorporates a physicality and sense of proximal space that is in part defined by the established socio-cultural responses of the prevailing community to the meta-geographic and urban landscape that the body lives in. This naturally impacts on how performers work in rehearsal, the decisions they make, the ways they use their bodies, and the ways in which those bodies are read by audiences.

What were those differences, how did they relate to the socio-historic, cultural responses that each cast had grown up in, and what does that mean for how we consider the body in performance?

---

3   *Tashunga*, Dir. Nils Gaup, 1996

134

Physical Difference in Rehearsal

The rehearsals I attended were for Nationaltheatret's 2007 production of Ludvig Holberg's *Erasmus Montanus*, directed by Gábor Zsámbéki in Oslo, and Griffin Theatre Company's premiere production of Katherine Thompson's *King Tide*, directed by Patrick Nolan in Sydney. I identified four major areas of divergence:

1. Actor-to-actor communication

2. Personal space/proxemics

3. Need to do/need to move[4]

4. Labanian weight-in-the-body.

Of these, actor-to-actor communication and need to do/need to move were heavily influenced by such crucial elements as directorial style, rehearsal space, rehearsal period, economic security, and the structure of hierarchical power relationships within each company. Proxemic space and Labanian weight in the body were not as determined by these factors, and could be at least partially ascribed to the way each actor had embodied place; had 'learnt' place in their understanding and use of their bodies.

Case Study 1: Proxemic Space

The opposing tendencies actors had with regard to personal space – in terms of being close to each other in the performance area – became a directorial issue in both productions.

Throughout Erasmus Montanus, *the actors continually made choices to move away from each other where possible. If instructed to enter the performance area together, all would choose to move apart once the opportunity arose. Within sequences where Gábor asked them to come together, many exhibited a 'shuffling' motion where a static, bodies-close-together stance would be punctuated by a small weight change forward, followed by two to three small steps backward.*[5]

---

4   In my observation the Norwegian actors all required a physical action to define their time on stage, constantly asking 'What shall I do?' and using props to do it. The Australians constantly moved: they couldn't stand still even when asked to, until later in the rehearsals when they apparently felt more secure with the play.

5   Actors Henrik, Thorbjørn, Finn, Erik, Håkon, Christian, Marian all exhibited this movement at various times throughout the rehearsals.

Gábor first commented on the issue of distance early in rehearsal when he spoke to actors Finn and Håkon: "You are diluting the power of your unity by moving apart. The scene requires you operate together" (Hope, 2007). He repeated the essence of this comment to the whole company in his notes following a run of the play, commenting that the tendency to move apart was reducing the dramatic effect of the blocking,[6] and maintained a reference to being aware of on-stage distances as an ongoing note from hereon through to opening night.

All the Norwegian actors showed a marked preference for maintaining physical distance from each other when rehearsing.

Speaking with Gørild, a Norwegian actor working outside the *Erasmus Montanus* production, on-stage proxemic space was put in a national context. Whilst studying with Lecoq, Gørild had become aware that both her own and her Norwegian compatriot students' perception of personal space was more expansive than that of students from other countries. Gørild suggested that my observations of extended proximal space on the rehearsal floor in *Erasmus Montanus* were indicative of a specifically Norwegian sense of personal space.[7]

In Sydney, Patrick Nolan had the opposite concern.

Kathryn, the youngest member of the cast, was repeatedly asked to be aware of not "closing off" from the audience. In the week following a concerted effort by Patrick to concentrate on spatial distance between characters, I heard Kathryn stopping herself closing in on co-actor Toni with the whispered words: "Too close, too close," whilst actor Masa whispered a similar self-note: "Oh, I'm starting to go towards, remember away, away" (Hope, 2007a).

Whilst the *King Tide* actors played with proxemic space during the improvisation of scenes, their tendency as the rehearsals progressed was to move *toward* each other on the rehearsal floor. The inclination to congregate was common to all.

Patrick commented on the danger of making the use of the playing space too intimate, on "shutting out" the audience from sightlines and audibility (the actors were prone to lowering vocal levels when close to each other),

---

6   'Blocking' is the choreography of the actors on stage; when and where they move.

7   That is, a large distance in respect to that which I am used to and, in Gørild's training experience, a distance considered large by non-Norwegian co-students.

and "of getting too close, too clustered" (Hope, 2007a).

Whilst the actors played with spatial formations, it was noticeable that physical closeness was a choice made for actions encompassing a range from confrontation to seduction, and that left to themselves (as they often were), actors would tend to *end* a sequence by closing the gap between each other, regardless of the nature of the emotional transaction occurring.

Within the rehearsal room, the *King Tide* actors would sit together in a tight cluster for notes and for tea-break, in contrast to the *Erasmus Montanus* company, who sat singly or in couples. Nevertheless, when the subject of personal space was brought up, the *King Tide* actors stated that Australians had a *large* personal space: that their physicality was "big" because of the "open" landscape. The *notion* of personal space seemed to relate to a personal notion of physicality within a spacious landscape, rather than the limits of comfort in closeness to another human being. Kathryn spoke of loving the open-air lifestyle, and missing the smaller, friendlier urbanity of Brisbane; others (Katherine [writer], Anita, Russell) talked about personal space in terms of wanting to live in the crowded areas of the city for the sense of human presence and activity. Their preferred mode of living appeared to be in highly populated areas, a mode of living one would assume to be in opposition to the concept of living in a "spacious landscape".

In both productions, the operation of personal space between actors – the way in which they arranged themselves in terms of the amount of distance between themselves as physical beings – demonstrated itself similarly both on and off the performance area.

The observed contrast between initial and ongoing choices regarding bodily proximity in both sets of rehearsals was a constant variation. Several potential explanations for these differences immediately present themselves. The *King Tide* actors were continually in each other's presence during rehearsal; the *Erasmus Montanus* cast were not. This would suggest a greater breakdown of physical primary tensions[8] amongst the actors in the *King Tide* production. Yet the *Erasmus Montanus* actors were part of an ensemble that worked together consistently; the *King Tide* cast were

---

8   Primary tension is that tension experienced in a group which has not yet established its own social boundaries.

freelancers. The *Erasmus Montanus* cast socialised together outside the rehearsals, whilst the *King Tide* cast were less personally familiar with each other. One would expect the *Erasmus Montanus* cast to be at least equally at ease with each other as the *King Tide* actors.

Performance Studies academic Gay McAuley and Nationaltheatret actor Henrik Rafaelson argued that the spatial choices the actors made could be explained by their performative desire to 'fill' the rehearsal/performance space, rather than by their unconscious allegiance to a national proxemic trait. If this were the case, one could expect an opposite result. *Erasmus Montanus* worked with a nearly completed set from day one, so that the space was in many ways constricted; whilst *King Tide* utilised an almost empty set, opening up the space and inviting it to be filled.

There were national, socio-cultural and physically embodied factors at play in the use of proximal space between actors; but before we look at these, we will consider the second major comparative difference.

Case Study 2: Weight in the Body

This consideration first became apparent when the Hungarian composer arrived to work with the *Erasmus Montanus* company.

László Sáry was a slight man, stooped over, his arms held close to the sides but not locked in at the elbows. His gestures were short, his arms never quite stretched all the way out, and his fingers in constant motion:

> *Seeing him in pit & Anne Marit & Per on stage – physical presence so different – composer small, held, little space taken; AM & Per larger, physically more open, arms, legs, facial gestures take more space.* (Hope, [08/08] 2007).

I watched László work with Anne Marit on a musical section:

> *13:48 – AM stands with hands on head and explains it is difficult, she is unsure – composer asks her to 'try' and waves his hands and fingers at her, his hands twirling in little circles – AM stands still, hands on head...*

> *14:00 – AM talks with composer again, her gestures strong, weighted, his flighty, floating – like sign language.* (Hope, [08/08] 2007).

László, in Labanian terms, came across as a *lightweight flicker*, and his presence alerted me to the fact that I had not seen any *lightweight* actors on the stage.[9] I began to observe the actors in terms of how they carried their weight.

Finn, in his final scene of humiliation, adopted a posture bent at the waist and knees, but maintained a solid, heavy stance in his legs and feet. Håkon, whose character was low status, had a *strong-weight pressing* quality, moving forward from the hips in a straight, steady gait, with careful, planted steps. Thorbjørn, who had been asked to be open and light, was instead heavy in his walk, continually returning to a bow-legged gait with a stamping footstep, heavily swung arms, and a pressing-from-the-hips stride. Henrik practised a pigeon-toed stance with a top-heavy quality and a swaying motion that, again, led to heavily placed footsteps, with weight bearing into the ground. Anne Marit was naturally *strong-weight*, as was Per. The cast choices, or their natural tendencies, all leant toward a *strong-weight, direct, sustained quality*. It appeared that all were using the same sense of weighted presence that pervaded their physicality, showing itself in space-taking physical stances and walks.

In contrast, Kathryn from the *King Tide* company told Masa in the second week of rehearsal that she had been asked to wear more solid clothes and shoes in order to become more grounded. Masa replied that Patrick had asked him, too, to become more grounded. "We'll be a bunch of grounded people," said Kathryn.

The 'lighter' quality of bodily presence amongst all the *King Tide* actors became clear as the actors began to work 'on the floor'. During the readings, Anita had developed a '*slashing*' arm and hand movement style that she used when gesticulating; once standing and moving, her body took on a swaying motion that suited the use of her arms. Gillian swayed from foot to foot, and her arms flicked and floated around chest level, the hands making circular motions as she spoke, giving her a light and sharp presence. Masa would often fidget, hands playing with his clothes or hair, and he made rapid choices between sitting, standing or moving around the rehearsal area. Kathryn gave the impression of constantly floating. Her hands would

---

9   See 'Rudolf Laban' in the Glossary for an explanation of these terms and, for more detail, see Adrian (2002).

sail into the air above her head when she spoke, and her legs would twine around each other or be held behind her back. Toni used a lot of facial, hand and finger gesticulation. She jogged on the spot and raised herself on tiptoes to find the energy and/or intent of the moment. In the third week she discussed with Patrick her difficulty in finding the *weight* for her character, and also decided to rehearse in heavier shoes, to give herself a sense of groundedness.

The *King Tide* actors were generally more *lightweight, indirect,* and *quick-sudden* in Labanian terms: their initial physical presence less grounded than that of the *Erasmus Montanus* company, and it affected how they approached their roles.

In both cases, the physical presentation of character – and therefore the messages sent, received and negotiated between actor and audience – were in part defined by what appeared to be nationally ubiquitous choices of proximity and body weight in a Labanian sense. What kind of model can we use to consider how and why those choices are made?

'Self', Perception and Embodied Place

If we consider a concept of 'self" that unites body, pre-reflective and reflective consciousness in the one unit of being, then that being – Zarrilli's (2004) bodymind or Gibbs's (2008) body-brain-world – exists in a tactile-kinaesthetic relationship with its given world, such that the 'self' is in a state both of constant communication with that world, and constant delineation between 'self' and world. The understanding of 'self' is dependent on the understanding of world.

The world is a given in terms of the way the 'self' as a bodymind interacts with it, on a physical and perceptive level. As Casey (2001) writes, 'place' is the immediate environment of the lived body, and that immediate environment is what the lived body must interact with. The perceptive level of interaction, however, is subject not only to the tactile-kinaesthetic explorations or demands of bodymind, world and others, it is also subject to the *shape* of perception as presented within a socio-historico-cultural context.

The bodymind, then, develops a sense of immediate environment – of place – through both physical interaction and socio-cultural presentation.

Maurice Merleau-Ponty's Fundiering Model (1962) suggests a disarmingly simple way to envision how this conjoint habituation of place shapes itself as an element of perception. The communication, interpretation and response of 'self' and world can be seen as *emanating* from the perceived, experienced world, but *sedimenting* itself through the communal world and through shared emotional reactions within a shared community. Merleau-Ponty's phenomenological lived body in the lived world is recognised in this way as a *social* as well as a physical, sensual being; indeed, the social, physical and sensual are all intersensory parts of the unified 'self'-in-the-world. The experienced and socially filtered, sedimented response to lived place and lived landscape becomes an organic part of the lived body; it becomes a pre-reflective response that is a major component of the bodymind. These habituated responses that help define the 'self' in terms of the world, show place, landscape and 'self' as inextricably interconnected and co-defined within human consciousness.

The relevance of this to observations of proxemic space and Labanian body weight in the rehearsals I attended will, I hope, be clear. The actors all brought a socio-culturally, pre-defined and embodied understanding of lived and socially filtered responses to their lived world/landscape into rehearsal, and referenced those pre-reflective responses *as a given* to understand, interpret and create the *imagined* world. The lived worlds of each individual actor, along with the intricacies of each individual life history, diverged in myriad ways; but it is possible to look at the macro-world surrounding the actors – the socio-historico-cultural response and/or construction toward the project of living – to begin to investigate what influence, if any, that response/construction had on the kinds of variation in observed rehearsal presentation.

Norway

Film and Media Studies Professor Bjørn Sørenssen (2001) traces a cultural understanding of 'being Norwegian' that involves an element of being physically involved with the land in a nationally understood concept of a 'healthy outdoor life', which has its own term: *friluftsliv*. This sense of Norwegian 'connection' to the landscape – or at least to a projected romantic version of the landscape (see Setten, 2004) – is sustained in

Stråth's political analysis of the role of the peasant in Norwegian society (2004), and in Müller (2007) and Vittersø's (2007) discussion of the historical and contemporary importance of *hytteliv*[10] in Norwegian life and national identity. The resulting socio-historically constructed sense of Norwegian individuality as a version of the self-sufficient human being working and playing with(in) the landscape (and climate) becomes apparent from early rural organisation through to polar explorer Fridtjof Nansen's nationally famous promotion of the 'simple life outdoors', and on to the present day. *Friluftsliv* involves *strong-weight* activities: hiking, skiing, water collection and so on, and, in the Norwegian milieu, is defined by singular or very small-group physical isolation. Considered as a series of ubiquitous national characteristics, these socio-cultural edifices show as a superb 'fit' when applied to the Labanian *strong-weight* tendencies of the Norwegian cast, and also to their (relatively) extended sense of proxemic space.

Australia

Australia's colonial past informs the Australian people's socio-historico-cultural approach to the continent. The image of the land as a narrow rim of inhabitability with a mystical and hostile desert centre predominates in many of the representations of Australia, from art and film (Haynes, 1998) to literature (Haynes, 1998; Köster, 1991), to politics and the History Wars (Howitt, 2001; Arrow 2007). The cultural imagination accepts the icon of the continent as a symbol of identification (McGrath in Haynes, 1998), but removes itself from being part of that identity; in the cultural imaginary, an understanding of the continent is in many ways the mystical property of the indigenous people. The continent itself is 'othered', and the cultural aspirations of its peoples elsewhere-placed. This assessment is supported by a consideration of the history of the policy of Multiculturalism, wherein an underlying Euro/Anglo-centric cultural allegiance is uncovered.[11] Similarly, a discussion of the aspirations of inner-city dwellers in Sydney by both Shaw (2006) and Rofe (2009) corroborates an urban Australian 'othering'

---

10 *Hytteliv* basically refers to holiday life in a hut in the wilderness, a popular Norwegian form of holiday recreation.

11 See for example Castles *et al*. (1988) and Galligan and Roberts (2003).

of the continent's landscape and climate, and a cultural and visual aspiration towards the opposite global hemisphere – specifically Europe (London, Paris) and America (New York).

This sense of what I would categorise as displacement was perpetuated in discussions with the *King Tide* cast. The 'real' of the continent was often described as desert (rather than tropics, mountains or rainforests), and as belonging to, and understood by, the indigenous people. Preferred places of living were culturally Anglo-European. The concept of 'Australian-ness' was largely seen as something negative, and disassociated with on an individual level. The incidence of Labanian weight use – in this case *lightweight* – has clear associations with a lack of physical/emotional connection to the projected, understood (and presumably pre-reflective) concept of the 'real' Australia. The (relatively) contracted use of proximal space similarly appears to 'fit' the equally contracted nature of the spread of the population, and of its relationship to the landscape as hostile. The people, considering the landscape to be vast, unmanageable and hostile, huddle together.

The consistent differences observed in Labanian weight and use of proximal space between both casts are, I propose, clearly influenced by socio-historico-cultural responses to landscape and climate, and the way these impact on individual, tactile-kinaesthetic responses to landscape and climate. More than this, they can be seen in the light of responses to the *understood* and *projected* notions of the greater lived world, as in the Norwegian Romantic 'simple life outdoors' or the Australian Colonial 'continent as other'. Embodied landscape and climate is seen here in a Merleau-Pontian phenomenological sense, where Merleau-Ponty's vision of the 'self' as 'flesh of the world' can be considered in terms of Zarilli's bodymind *in* the world. The whole bodymind unity of 'self'hood is formed by its constantly adaptive intercommunication with the lived-in world, seen and filtered through the communal world, institutionalisation, sedimentation, and a socially and environmentally enhanced (or at least moulded) reception of perception. The embodiment of landscape and climate through this multi-filter affects the way the emotive, sensual bodymind interacts with its physical world.

In a performative environment, the bodymind is imaginatively removed from the lived world, but asked to refer to engagement in that world in order to create another, imaginary world. In such an environment, reflection on the pre-reflective attributes of body-weight connection to the world is entertained; and the space of interaction with other beings is re-negotiated. It is highly likely that the initial, widespread prevailing socio-cultural qualities of body-weight use (or emotive/cognitive investment in connection to the land) and proxemic space (or emotive/cognitive investment in individual spatial requirements) will be adopted as the default position. This, I believe, is what I observed during the rehearsals of *Erasmus Montanus* in Oslo, and *King Tide* in Sydney.

This may appear to be a deterministic outcome. Yet as Merleau-Ponty points out in *Phenomenology of Perception* (1962: 253), we can never 'know' an object or thing in its entirety; we can never see the whole of the object/thing from a God's-eye position encompassing all its perspectival angles, all its history, all its permutations: we are limited by our temporality and our perspectival physicality from ever fully 'knowing' any object/thing/other. The world the actor/cast/production creates in performance is limited to the world that can be imagined by that actor/cast/production at that time. It is the world as known to the limited extent that the performers/creators know their own world. The outcome may appear deterministic simply because the reality is deterministic.

Nevertheless, the idea that any performance is heavily indebted to such factors as the specific tactile-kinaesthetic, socio-historico-cultural embodiment of landscape and environment *expands* our ability to know our world. For the outside viewer, whose physically, sensately known, habituated and perceived world is similar-but-divergent, those differences in response and interpretation subtly communicated in body and interaction must surely affect how the viewer then continues to perceive their own world. The similar-but-divergent 'truths' of the world – of different lived bodies in same-yet-different lived worlds – become part of Merleau-Ponty's experience of dehiscence, of a peeling back of the flesh of the world to reveal a new, wider knowledge of world and 'self'. Difference in this view becomes learning: a part of the project of living. We may be flesh of the world, and the world is one huge body.

My own actor-training involved a process of eliminating one set of (personal) physical habits by imposing another (somewhat more ubiquitous) set, defined by particular movement techniques and responses: a process which has been colloquially termed the 'break them down, build them up' technique. Perhaps an alternative way to approach the training of the body is to first investigate and isolate the socio-culturally learnt aspects of its place-memory: to familiarise the 'self' with what is based in learnt body memory in order to consciously transcend socially coded habits and movement patterns. Such an approach would allow a conscious understanding of how and why the body-self works in a particular way in space and place, and would facilitate any chosen changes as well as promote a performative understanding and appreciation of those unique elements specific to the individual.

In my own experience, the demands of living in Norway and working in Norwegian film and theatre have inculcated themselves into my acting/living practice in terms of my physicality, my interpretation of events, and my sources of affective, emotional and sensory memory. My embodied world has expanded: my cognisance of immediate lived world, my sense of identity within locality, my connection to and understanding of my own body-map: my very understanding of world, and therefore, I propose, of 'self', has expanded. How can this not be part of my performed presentation of imaginary, yet shared referential worlds?

As Lewis writes: '...there can be no embodiment without emplacement... places and bodies co-construct each other...' (Lewis, 2010: 71). The body is not a unit unto itself: it is a co-dependent, learnt construct. Training the body surely requires that the body be understood in terms of its learnt construction.

Dr. Nicholas Hope has worked as an actor since 1989. He won an Australian Film Institute award for Best Actor for his role as Bubby in the film *Bad Boy Bubby*, was nominated for Best Supporting actor in the Norwegian Amanda Awards for his performance in *En Dag Til I Solen*, and continues to work in film, theatre and television around the world. He completed his PhD in Performance Studies at The University of Sydney, 2010. He teaches Directing Actors for Film at the International Film School Sydney, and is Head of Acting at the International Screen Academy, Sydney.
www.nicholashope.net
hopeproductions@nicholashope.net

Bibliography

Adrian, B. (2002) 'An Introduction to Laban Movement Analysis for Actors: A Historical, Theoretical, and Practical Perspective' in Potter, N. (ed.) *Movement For Actors*, New York: Allworth Press

Arrow, M. (2007) '"That history should not have ever been how it was": The Colony, Outback House, and Australian History', *Film and History*, 37 (1): 54-65

Casey, E. S. (2001) 'Between Geography and Philosophy: What Does It Mean to Be in the Place-World?' *Annals of the Association of American Geographers*, 91 (4): 683-693

Castles, S., Kalantzis, M., Cope, W. and Morrissey, M. (1988) *Mistaken Identity: Multiculturalism And the Demise of Nationalism in Australia*, Sydney: Pluto Press

Galligan, B. and Roberts, W. (2003) 'Australian Multiculturalism: Its Rise and Demise' in *Australasian Political Studies Association Conference*. University of Tasmania, Hobart: www.utas.edu.

Gibbs, R. W. (2008) 'Images Schemas in Conceptual Development: What Happened to the Body?', *Philosophical Psychology* 21 (2): 9

Haynes, R. D. (1998) *Seeking the Centre: the Australian Desert in Literature, Art and Film*, Cambridge: Cambridge University Press

Hope, N. (2011) 'Embodied Landscape: the place of geography in the actor's creation of character', *Body, Space and Technology*, Vol. 10, Issue 2, p.1

_____ (2010) *Inner Place: The Impact of Embodied Landscape on Actor Decisions in Rehearsal: An Actor's perspective*, PhD University of Sydney, Department of Performance Studies

_____ (2007) Unpublished Field Notes: *Erasmus Montanus*, Oslo.

_____ (2007a) Unpublished Field Notes: *King Tide*, Sydney.

Holberg, L. and Hjelseth, R. P. (2005) *Erasmus Montanus: av Ludvig Holberg.*, Molde, Norway: Teatret Vårt.

Howitt, R. (2001) 'Frontiers, Borders, Edges: Liminal Challenges to the Hegemony of Exclusion', *Australian Geographical Studies* 39 (2): 233-245

Johnstone, A. A. (1992) 'The Bodily Nature of the Self or What Descartes Should Have Conceded Princess Elizabeth of Bohemia' in Sheets-Johnstone, M. (ed.) *Giving the Body Its Due*, Albany, NY: SUNY Press

Köster, E. J. (1991) *Operating From Bastard Territory: Attitudes Toward the Motherland And The Colonial self in Four Australian and Canadian Novelists*, London, Ont: English University of Western Ontario

Lewis, J. L. (2010) *The Anthropology of Cultural Performance,* Unpublished

Merleau-Ponty, M. (1962) *Phenomenology of Perception,* London: Routledge and Kegan Paul

_____ (1964) *The Primacy of Perception : and other essays on phenomenological psychology, the philosophy of art, history, and politics: Northwestern University studies in phenomenology and existential philosophy,* Evanston, IL: Northwestern University Press

_____ (2004) *The World of Perception,* London: Routledge

Müller, D. K. (2007) 'Second Homes in the Nordic Countries: Between Common Heritage and Exclusive Commodity', *Scandinavian Journal of Hospitality and Tourism* 7 (3): 193-201

Parviainen, J. (2002) 'Bodily Knowledge: Epistemological Reflections on Dance', *Dance Research Journal* 34 (1): 11-26

Rofe, M. W. (2009) 'Globalisation, Gentrification and Spatial Hierarchies in and beyond New South Wales: the Local/Global Nexus', *Geographical Research* 47 (3): 292-305

Schama, S. (1995) *Landscape and Memory,* London: HarperCollins

Setten, G. (2004) 'The habitus, the rule and the moral landscape', *Cultural Geographies* (11): 389-415

Shaw, W. S. (2006) 'Sydney's SoHo Syndrome? Loft living in the urbane city', *Cultural Geographies* 13: 182-206

Shilling, Chris (2005) 'Contemporary Bodies' in Featherstone, M. (ed.) *The Body in Culture, Technology, and Society,* 47-54 London: Sage

Sørenssen, B. (2001) 'Radical Romanticism in Scandinavian Documentary: The Norwegian Nature "Meme" in "For harde livet"', *Film History* 13 (1): 50-57

Stråth, B. (2004) 'Nordic Modernity: Origins, Trajectories and Prospects', *Thesis Eleven* (77:5): 5-22

Thomas, M. (2003) *The Artificial Horizon: Imagining the Blue Mountains,* Melbourne: Melbourne University Press

Thompson, Katherine (2007) *King Tide,* Sydney: Currency Press

Vitterso, Gunnar (2007) 'Norwegian Cabin Life in Transition', *Scandinavian Journal of Hospitality and Tourism* 7 (3): 266-280.

Zarilli, P. B. (2004) 'Toward a Phenomenological Model of the Actor's Embodied Modes of Experience', *Theatre Journal* 56:4 (Dec): 653-666

The Kinetic Body

Foot, Memory and Dispositions of the Body in Performance

Arya Madhavan and Sreenath Nair

Abstract

Performance is a bodily scheme of practice that connects the real and unreal – the physical and symbolic – worlds. Foot is the *modus operandi* that connects space and time in performance through movements enabling perceptual *trance*-formations between the *real* and *unreal* worlds. Foot may be seen as synonymous with movement; a movement that is capable of affecting the mind outside of all representation. Physically, being the terminal part of the leg below the ankle joint, foot is the active presence, located in the physical space and time through which the symbolic world of performance unfolds in the spectacle of the body. The chapter focuses on exploring the performative dynamics of rhythm and breathing in the context of foot and on investigating the nature of the actor/dancer's *presence* through a range of vocabularies and practices derived from Indian martial arts and classical Sanskrit theatre known as *Kudiyattam*. Foot, as the apparatus of movement, generates kinetic energy employing spatial and temporal properties of the body. It is also the embodiment of feeling in the sense that the foot positions and pathways render the collective ceremony of bodily 're-collections'.

"The body believes in what it plays at: it weeps if it mimes grief. It does not represent what it performs, it does not memorise the past, it *enacts* the past, bringing it back to life." (Bourdieu, 1990: 73)

Bridget is a contemporary dancer. She has long years of experience as a dancer and her training had been in Western contemporary dance techniques. She is aware that her movement culture is conditioned by the styles of dance that she is trained in. She realises that this could be seen as a limitation if she wants to work internationally as a choreographer. Therefore she decides to explore movement practice in Asian cultures so that she can develop an understanding of the non-western approach to bodily practice. Bridget believes that this will equip her to expand her resources as a dancer and prepare her to engage in, and develop, new and innovative choreographic models.

Bridget decides to work with us. It is the first time that her body has encountered anything 'new' in terms of movement. Bridget is slightly nervous because she does not know what to expect. She comes to the studio. Straight away we start with movement work.

Performance is a bodily scheme of practice. It connects the 'real' and 'unreal', the physical and symbolic, the objective and subjective, the fictive and narrative, and the verbal and gestural dimensions of the body. Performance as a "practice is always oriented towards practical functions" (*ibid*: 52) of the body. In this sense, a performance, on the one hand, is 'realism' in relation to the skeletal and muscular structures of the body, which includes rhythm, movement and the entire corporeal schema of the body (Merleau-Ponty, 1962: 230). On the other hand, a performance enables an act of escaping of the body from the objective relationships that it creates with the orchestration of other bodies and objects in space and time.

The body in performance, therefore, is always about 'a' body other than the actor's and, hence, it is fictive and an object of perception. This inevitable disappearance of the 'objective body' is the essential temporal ingredient that generates the symbolic presence (*opus operatum*) in a performance. The performance, therefore, is the site of the dialectics of the body in action. It is the domain of constant *trance*-formations of the body embedded in endless movements "without falling back into subjectivism" (Bourdieu, 1990: 52): the movement only creates another movement, not the concept.

The disappearance of the objective body in a performance, in this sense, does not generate 'lack' as we understand it in the discourse of linguistic deconstruction, but causes the emergence of another body, which is perceptually kinetic and visually symbolic. A performance, therefore, is a *trance*-formative world, existing in between the 'double' appearance of the body – the biological body of the performer and the fictive representation of the body – within a single unit of somatic framework. It is not the linguistic model of presence and absence, but rather the performance model that enables the co-existence of multiple bodies in a performance: the performer and what is being performed.

Foot is the *modus operandi* that connects the 'double' appearance of the body in space and time through movements enabling perceptual *trance*-formations between the *real* and *unreal*. Foot is the active presence, located in the physical space and time through which the symbolic world of performance unfolds in the spectacle of the body. Physically being the terminal part of the leg, below the ankle joint, foot is always about standing positions and movements. It is about the basic functionality of movement, rhythm and pace: foot is "spontaneity without consciousness" (*ibid*: 56), which is embedded in the corporeal logic of action.

Foot is historically considered in western choreography as the position and balance of the body. Pierre Rameau makes some interesting observations about the body position in dance as follows:

> "What is termed a position is nothing more than a separation or bringing together of the feet according to a fixed distance, while the body is maintained upright and in equilibrium without any appearance of constraint, whether one walks, dances, or comes to a stop." (Rameau, 1970: 5).

Rameau proposes five fundamental body positions that he considers indispensable and unbreakable rules in dance.[1] Insistently, Rameau further argues that the 'design' of the body postures in dance is as important as music to a composer of ballets, and nothing is more important than these five positions in maintaining 'the body in a graceful attitude' (*ibid*: 5). The body positions differ only in accordance with the changes of the leg and feet and therefore, for Rameau, these five feet positions are 'indispensable rules which must be kept' (*ibid*: 5). It is very clear that Rameau is talking about an intimate physical connectivity between the body positions and the feet as a fundamental source of the visibility of 'grace' (presence) in the dancer's body.

---

1   Pierre Rameau's body positions originated from the work of Monsieur Beauchamps who built the foundation for the art of dance. Beauchamps was the director of the Académie Royale de Dance, composer and superintendent of the King's Ballet in 1661 and Maître de Ballet of the Académie Royale de Musique in 1671. He continued in this post until 1687 and died in 1695.

These five positions of the feet became part of the European 'balletic heritage' and we see the positions of the feet and the leg gestures forming the fundamental principles of Labanotation. Foot generates movements and the "clear placement of the feet requires clear indications in changing from one position to another" (Guest, 2005: 52). Foot denotes a number of functions in Labanotation referring to 'standing legs', 'moving legs' and 'rhythmic legs', which are operative tools, repetitive in nature, as well as being a signifying device constitutive of the very structure and meaning of the dance. Open and closed positions of the feet, their transitions "in terms of motion away from the previous point of support" (*ibid*: 58) and their retention of a previous point create the movements in dance. Movement produces new positions and the body returns to destinations and positions between movements. Leg 'swings', 'bends', 'jumps' and 'beats' on the dancing floor while holding the space in a variety of levels and dimensions.

In modern choreography, as Susan Leigh Foster observes, all the movements share the same fundamental properties of shape, rhythm and force demonstrating the possibilities of shaping the body as a three-dimensional object in space (Foster, 2011: 49). The structuring principles of modern choreography, therefore, in many ways, are based on phrases like repetition, inversion, amplification or contraction, which are terms related to movements, directly or indirectly associated with the positions and movements of feet. Nevertheless, the positioning of dancers' feet in Classical Indian dance and martial arts appears to be functioning in a different manner.

FOOT

Today Bridget is taught the basic feet and leg positions of KUDIYATTAM. She is advised to keep her knee bent and feet sideways throughout. Her back is upright with a slight curve at the base of the spine. Bridget performs full trunk rotations while maintaining this posture. She struggles to maintain the posture for more than a minute. She slowly realises the "pain similar to walking on the tip of a needle" central to Indian movement culture. She asks about the intentions behind such painful physical postures and exercises. It is explained that foot leads every other limb-movement in a performance and that the training prepares foot to serve this task.

Foot is a synonym for movement: a movement that is capable of affecting the mind outside of all representation. Representation is mediation, but the movement is direct and always takes place outside of representation. As Gilles Deleuze observes, "movement itself [is] a work, without interposition; of substituting direct signs for mediate representations; of inventing vibrations, rotations, whirlings, gravitations, dances or leaps which directly touch the mind" (Deleuze, 2001: 8). Dance/Performance is 'real' movement and foot 'extracts' the body into motion. Foot repeats in a performance and, therefore, movement is repetition: repetition, not in the sense of 'repeating' the same action, but in the sense of being devoid of representation. Foot as repetition takes the dancer's body from one fixed position to another through kinetic sequences of body movements. This repetition is not the 'repeating' of the same but always terminates in new positions in space: the dancer never returns to a previous position once the dance has begun since time is progressive. Foot, in this sense, is "pure force" and "terrible power". It creates patterns of "dynamic lines in space" that speak a language before words, (*ibid*: 10) and delivers gestures that organise the movement of the body before a performance takes place. Foot as the apparatus of movement connects the *physis* and *psyche* in pure force of kinetic energy.

Foot is considered to be a kinetic tool in the *NATYASASTRA*, in relation to rhythm, movement and the entire bodily schema of the performer. In Sanskrit, the language in which the *Natyasastra* was composed, *Chari* means movement. As a discipline, movement is discussed extensively in the *Natyasastra* over four lengthy chapters: the fourth chapter classifies the 108 foot and leg positions (*Karana*) and 32 basic units of dance movements (*Angahara*); the eleventh chapter is about training 32 basic foot movements; the twelfth chapter is about choreographing movement sequences (*Mandala*) such as war and duel; and in the thirteenth chapter we see a lexical narrative of the relationship between meaning and movements showing how each movement defines the character of objects and persons in a performance. The description includes the depiction of animals such as horses, elephants and birds; objects such as chariots, planes and boats; motions such as floating and falling from the sky; characters such as the drunken man, madman and courtesan. Moreover, the chapter explains how social status and gender classifications are defined by bodily positions such as sitting, standing and lying down.

Foot creates different sets of temporal relations of the body in the *Natyasastra*. Several sets of these leg and hand positions – more than eight according to the *Natyasastra* – and their subsequent movements create the basic dance units (Pisharoti, 1987: 147). Beyond the level of leg and hand positions, which form the basic vocabulary of dance movement, four types of movements of the limbs, spin, upward and downward movements, twist and rotation are mentioned. All these minor movements connect a range of combined movements of the hands and legs in dance choreography (*ibid*: 188-89). According to the principles of movement explained by Bharatha, foot leads the body; more precisely, foot leads the hands and the hands lead the body (*ibid*: 396). The position of foot also defines the movements of the eye and the eyebrows. The *Natyasastra* lays down the foundations of a theory and practice of Indian performance studies for a period more than 2000 years (Vatsyayan, 1996: 26) and the key concept emerging from the discussion asserts the position of foot as a pivotal operative tool for the entire kinetic schema of the body in training and performance.

FOOT AND RHYTHM

The session today starts with 'springs'. Bridget is performing a series of 'springs' with intermittent breaks. This is followed by footwork set to certain rhythmic cycles. She stomps her feet to the varying tempos of highly meticulous rhythmic syllables. Bridget is excited but confused. She has lots of questions, but she is asked to continue with her footwork instead. She is also advised to chant the rhythmic syllables when she stomps so that there is better co-ordination between the upper and lower part of her body. From time to time she is asked to relax silently in stillness. Her body slowly becomes the vibrating rhythm. Bridget is now calm and focused.

In Indian performance studies, the body is a site of knowledge that reproduces thoughts and feelings through a schema of systematically codified techniques of corporeal practice. The performer's body in *Kudiyattam* is inherently extra-daily in the sense that there is nothing natural to the foot or leg movements. Foot movements and leg gestures perform a variety of kinetic functions in training and performance.

Foot is central to the physical regime of *Kudiyattam* training,[2] which functions on three distinct levels: 1) it builds up physical stamina to enable the actors to satisfy the extreme bodily demands required for the performance; 2) it develops a sense of rhythm and timing in relation to physical movements; and 3) it promotes flexibility, reflexivity and physical presence through various exercises. One of the significant foot-specific exercises is a series of one hundred springs that bring the feet very close to the forehead. Figure 1 shows the degree of bend the body is expected to maintain during this exercise.

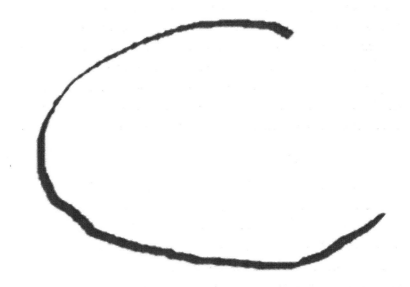

Figure 1: A graphic representation of the body in the *Kudiyattam* spring exercise.

---

2   The daily training sessions, conducted by the guru, typically start in the very early hours of the morning with rigorous physical training led by vocal rendering of the rhythmic syllables. The training period is extensive and it typically takes 6 to 8 years to become an actor. See for details: Sowle (1982) and Madhavan (2010).

Foot leads the rhythm in *Kudiyattam*. Since the percussion closely follows the performer's mimetic physical actions, facial expressions and hand gestures, the actor must acquire a comprehensive insight into various rhythmic structures and their impact on bodily motions during performance. Foot leaps, stomps and dances through the rhythmic cycles. Foot vibrates rhythm in its beats and pauses. A *Kudiyattam* performance takes place within a complex structure of various sequential patterns of rhythmic modulations.[3] Years of actor training prepare the performer to maintain an inner sense of rhythmic continuum unaffected by any external distractions. Here foot becomes an embodiment of rhythm and its kinetic modalities such as stomping, kicking, swinging, springing and stretching engage the body and mind actively with the physical and inner movements. To cite an example, one rhythmic leg exercise (*Kalsadhakam*) consists of beats of four, rendering *dhi- ta- ta- ta*.[4] The toes are joined and curled in, and knees are slightly bent outward. The leg movement consists of four stompings: the first two beats (*dhi-ta*) are in-steps that are the right and left stomping positions of legs in close spatial proximity, whereas the following two beats are right and left out-steps (*ta-ta*), forming a wider leg position. These four beats (*Tala*) form a single rhythmic orbit comprising meticulous stomping patterns with rhythmic variations. A strict time gap is observed between each stomp in any specific rhythmic orbit, performed in four progressively developing tempos (*Kala*).

The temporal structure and the sequential pattern of footwork is a cluster of complex networks of movements. Foot creates orbits of rhythm and movements, and each of these atomic structures consists of three complementary rhythmic orbits: the external phonic rhythmic orbit; the physical rhythmic orbit; and the internal mental rhythmic orbit. The external phonic orbit, which is the vocal articulation of the rhythm, maintains the overall duration of the footwork. The physical rhythmic orbit, which is created by the feet, generates movements of varying tempos,

---

3   There are 10 variations of rhythmic patterns used in *Kudiyattam*: Ekatalam, *Triputatala, Jhampatatala, Dhruvatala, Chempatatala, Atatala, Lakshmitala, Panchari, Madhyatala* and *Mallatala*. See more details in Nambiar (1996).

4   Vocal rendition (*vaythari*) forming different rhythmic syllables relating to various rhythmic cycles is a common practice in traditional Indian performances. This practice is named differently in different dance forms in India.

in arithmetical and geometrical patterns. Parallel to this is the inner rhythm, corresponding to the mental activity of the performer, which is the result of synthesising the external phonic and the physical rhythms. The inner rhythm is the nucleus, and foot infuses the continuum of rhythmic orbits through objective coordination of the spatial and temporal properties of the movements. Foot connects the internal and external, visible and the invisible (Merleau-Ponty, 1964: 164), vocal and corporeal and the mental and physical through the irresistible power of movement. Foot, therefore, "carves time in rhythm, dilating or contracting [the] actions" (Barba, 1991: 211).

The four major feet positions in *Kudiyattam* are (Figure 2) the bent knee posture (a), posture for active physical movement with the left foot in front and right foot behind (b), toes curled-in posture (c) and the feet position of a maid (d). The first two postures (a & b) are adopted by both male and female actors when performing characters of either gender. The third and fourth postures (c & d) are employed only to suggest female characters.[5]

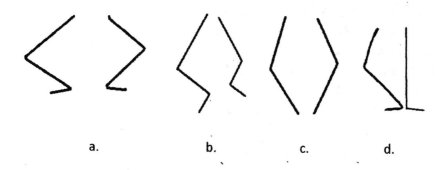

a.   b.   c.   d.

Figure 2: Four major feet positions in *Kudiyattam*.

---

5   In *Kudiyattam*, both female and male actors perform characters from either gender during *pakarnnattam*, which is multiple transformational acting. When male actors perform female characters during the play, a simple theatrical convention of tucking in one end of the costume, followed by the gender-specific feet position denotes the female character. There is no theatrical convention available for female performers to present male characters but feet positions, either bent-knee or the second feet position, are used to perform active movements when portraying male characters.

The alteration of foot positions in a performance, in this way, alters the audience's perception of gender roles assigned to characters. When a male performer takes the third posture (c) to represent a female character, a set of psycho-motor functions are evoked in him. The position of gaze is changed, the hand and arm position are altered and the total emotional response evoked by the male body relates to that of a female character.[6] The alteration of foot positions, therefore, evokes in the actor's body spontaneous, trained reflexes that are conditioned through years of training and performance. Altering the position of the feet is the stimulus that triggers the seemingly involuntary responses in the actor. As far as the audience are concerned, all that they see is the actor's voluntary alteration of the feet, which initiates some remembered and "restored" (Schechner, 1983: 164) reflexes, transmitting the illusion of a female character.

Foot, in this sense, is feeling embodied. It 're-places' the body in space and time into recurring postures that recall the bodily dispositions of thoughts and feelings. Foot positions and pathways render the collective ceremony of bodily 're-collections'. Each positioning of the foot will bring another series of bodily movements into play: the body has been trained rigorously in the past and the foot triggers those disciplined bodily memories. Foot *traces* the symbolic reappearance of the body as presence. The body becomes "the spontaneous orchestration of dispositions" (Bourdieu, 1990: 59) coordinated by the feet in a performance.

FOOT: BREATH AND PRESENCE

Today's movement session focuses on martial foot and presence. Bridget is taught to move through the axles of an imaginary circle of Tattu-Marma. Her circles are initially very big. She is a very tall person with long legs. So, every placing of her feet occupies a large space. She is continuously reminded to condense the space that she uses for each movement in the axle. Throughout the movement she is also asked to pay attention to her breathing. The movements slowly become condensed and her body slowly becomes energised. External breathing disappears. Sun shines in her eyes.

---

6   In the play *The Wedding of Arjuna and Subhadra* (*Subhadra Dhananjayam*) the hero, Prince Arjuna, enacts his lover, the Princess Subhadra, being dressed by her two maids. The feet position changes from posture 'b' to posture 'c' when the actor begins to show Subhadra.

Movement is a temporal property of the kinetic schema of the body. Foot moves parallel to the movement of breathing, and the body connects and synchronises these two movements – external and internal – through repetition of kinetic sequences of body movements. Foot and breathing are interconnected in this way and a movement of the foot begins with a movement of in-breath: foot mobilises the temporality of movement in the spatiality of breathing, meaning that each movement of the foot is extended into the spatiality of breathing. Each footstep is "temporally extended" (Heidegger, 1999: 4)[7] into the air and is mediated by the bipolar movement of breathing. In this way, foot defines the direction and intentionality of the movement making the body becoming 'a' body of constant becoming in the space and time. In *Tattu-Marma*[8] foot coordinates and synchronises the left and right legs and arms into brisk patterns of martial movements. Foot is martial in this sense and the defining characteristic of the martial art is the topography of the movements, creating the shape of a wheel (Figure 3).

---

7   In *An Introduction to Metaphysics* Martin Heidegger writes: "What is the temporal extension of a human life amid all the millions of years? Scarcely a move of the second hand, a breath."

8   *Tattu-Marma* is a rare form of Keralan martial art found in the region of Southern Travancore. It is neither popular among other schools of martial arts nor available beyond the strict family circles of the traditional *Marma* practitioners of Kerala. *Marma* is traditional physiotherapy based on medical knowledge of vital points of the body. It is mentioned in the traditional *Marma* manuscripts, supposedly written by a sage called Agastiya.

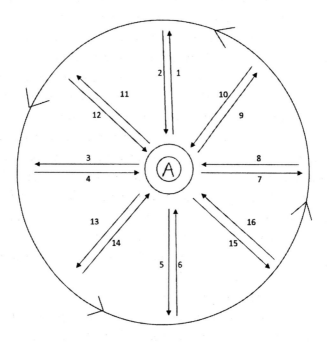

Figure 3: A=Axle. The second martial wheel of *Tattu-Marma* showing the bipolar
movements that create eight spokes made up of pathways.

Imagine the martial artist stands at the centre of the wheel at the axle
position (A). The movement begins from the axle position and each
direction of the movement creates each spoke in the martial wheel. A spoke
has two pathways and it consists of a bi-polar movement: the subsequent
movement forms an opposite direction as notated in the figures. A pathway
comprises two steps, moving away from the axle, coupled with a swift turn
of the body followed by an opposite movement towards the axle observing
the same rule.[9]

9　Two basic wheels of movements are used: the first wheel consists of four spokes and eight pathways of
movements while the second consists of eight spokes and, therefore, sixteen pathways of movements (see Figure 3). A third wheel, rarely used, consists of 16 spokes and 32 martial pathways. In order to create the third
wheel, a person requires an extraordinary sense of spatial awareness, considerable accuracy and precision in
their direction of movement, and incredible capacity of control over the body.

Foot with its "dance of opposition" (Barba, 1991: 176) takes the martial wheel in anti-clockwise direction. Left and right foot synchronise with left and right hand and the bipolar movement of the body synchronises with the bipolar movement of breathing. The left and right hand synchronise with left and right feet and the left and right sides of the body synchronise with various dimensions of the body and its martial postures. As the movement progresses through the offensive and defensive positions, a martial rhythm is created in the wheel. The bipolar movement of the feet coordinates with the bipolar movement of breathing and creates a single unity of rhythmic circles in the martial wheel. These rhythmic circles form an intact circle of physical and mental attention that makes the body present in the here and now within the circles of movements. The foot is placed at the axle position of the wheel; when foot moves the wheel moves and the martial movements create a field of kinetic energy in the wheel in motion. Breath moves the foot, and the rhythm of breathing follows the rhythm of foot: foot leads the body into revolving orbits of movements. Foot produces temporality through movements and the presence (*nira*) of the body is, therefore, rooted in the kinetics of breathing.

To conclude, foot remains the active presence in a performance practice connecting the physical and symbolic dimensions of the body through the corporeal logic of action through movement, rhythm and tempo. Foot, as the apparatus of movement, generates kinetic energy employing spatial and temporal properties of the body. It is also the embodiment of feeling in the sense that the foot positions and pathways render the collective ceremony of bodily 're-collections'. Underpinning the kinetics of breathing, foot produces temporality, which is the fundamental source of the presence of the body.

———————————

Dr. Arya Madhavan is a Lecturer in Drama at the Lincoln School of Performing Arts, University of Lincoln, UK. A trained performer of *Kudiyattam*, Madhavan's work and recent book (Madhavan, 2010) focus on analysing the contemporary relevance of *Kudiyattam* and re-assessing its performance techniques from the perspective of Performance Studies.
amadhavan@lincoln.ac.uk

Dr. Sreenath Nair is Senior Lecturer at the Lincoln School of Performing Arts, University of Lincoln, UK. Educated in India and UK, he received his PhD from the University of Aberystwyth, Wales in 2006. His research continues to explore embodied methodologies and practices of Kerala performance investigating the corporeal connections between medical, martial, spiritual and performance traditions in the region. Nair was awarded the Leverhulme Study Abroad Fellowship in 2011 and he took up the Scholar-in Residence appointment at Tisch School of the Arts at New York University in 2012. In 2013, he guest-edited a special issue of *Studies in South Asian Film and Media* on 'The Body'.
snair@lincoln.ac.uk

Bibliography

Barba, E. (1991) *A Dictionary of Theatre Anthropology: The Secret Art of the Performer*, R. Fowler (tr.), London: Routledge

Bourdieu, P. (1990) *The Logic of Practice*, Nice, R. (tr.), Cambridge: Polity Press

Deleuze, G. (2001) *Difference and Repetition*, Patton, P. (tr.), London: Continuum

Foster, S.L. (2011) *Choreographing Empathy: Kinesthesia in Performance*, London: Routledge

Guest, H. A. (2005) *Labanotation*, London: Routledge

Heidegger, M. (1999) *An Introduction to Metaphysics*, R. Manheim (tr.), New Delhi: Motilal Banarsidass

Madhavan, A. (2010) *Kudiyattam Theatre and the Actor's Consciousness*, Amsterdam: Rodopi

Merleau-Ponty, M. (1962) *The Phenomenology of Perception*, C. Smith (tr.), London: Routledge

_____ (1964) *The Primacy of Perception*, Evanston, IL: Northwestern University Press

Nair, S (2007) *Restoration of Breath: Consciousness and Performance* Amsterdam: Rodopi

Nambiar, P. K. N. (1996) 'Rhythm and Music', *Sangeet Natak*, 111-114: 101-12

Pisharoti, K.P. Narayana. (1987) (trans.) *Natyasastra of Bharatamuni* (Vol. I & II), Trichur: Kerala Sahitya Akademi

Rameau, P. (1970) *The Dancing Master*, Beaumont, C. W. (tr.), New York: Dance Horizon Press

Schechner, R. (1983) *Performative Circumstances From The Avant Garde to Ramlila*, Kolkata: Seagull Books

Sowle. S. (1982) *The Traditions, Training and Performance of Kutiyattam, Sanskrit Drama in South India* (Unpublished thesis), Berkeley, CA: University of California

Vatsyayan, K. (1996) *Bharata: The Natyasastra, New Delhi:* Sahitya Academi

The Cognitive Body

Using Embodied Cognition as a Tool for Performance-Making

Kate Hunter

Abstract

This chapter aims to depict and articulate a practice of 'embodied choice' as a constructive and compelling lens through which to examine a performance process.

The author's research incorporates neuroscientific principles of EMBODIED COGNITION to describe and articulate methods of physical DEVISING for performance. She is a devisor working in a post-dramatic context, so she situates this enquiry outside the formal theatrical conventions of 'script, actor and director'. Her work is 'non-fictive' in that she doesn't create character and narrative, but draws on autobiography, personal story, dreams and memories, and then manipulates the performance text to suit.

The author is curious about the body's processes of recall, choice and selection in performance-making. What procedures are taking place when one is devising, rehearsing and performing physical material? Are decisions made through the body, or the brain, or both? Can a language be created around these processes? How do we make up our minds?

In this chapter, she examines her own process of making work through the lens of neuroscientist Antonio Damasio's approach to embodied cognition. In particular, she refers to Damasio's model of the 'body-minded brain' as a potent framework within which a devising practice might be situated. She describes the way she uses movement improvisation as a component of her performance practice, with specific attention to the ordering, remembering, re-working, and manipulating of gesture, shape, dynamic and memory. The oral, spoken, written, embodied and performed material undergoes a manipulated trajectory from improvisation through rehearsal to performance. This process creates layered, complex work that is engaging, honest and clearly articulated.

I lie completely still, as if dead. I am on a blanket.
I look at the ceiling, and then I close my eyes.
I think about my earliest memory, and then my most recent memory. I consider
that my most recent memory would be recalling my earliest memory.
And then that becomes the most recent memory.
And so on and so on.

As an artist, I am compelled by notions of remembering and forgetting. I frequently wonder why I recall some things and forget others. I'm never quite sure why I include specific images, ideas, words, and gestures in my work, and leave others out.

Much of my performance training, over a 20-year period, has been underpinned by physical methodologies. From gymnastics, to circus and pratfalls, through street performance, into contact improvisation, Suzuki Training and Anne Bogart's Viewpoints, my trajectory of exploration has been grounded in and of the body. Along the way I have developed a practice of devising for performance that incorporates hybrid elements of recorded sound, writing and text, and physical gesture, through a method that generates and then re-works material in a constant and dynamic process of composition.

This journey of practice has led me to questions about the body's mysterious processes of recall, choice and selection, and a deeper enquiry into the nature of the brain and thought when one creates performance material. What exactly is occurring in the body, the brain and the mind when I am devising, rehearsing and performing physical material? Are decisions made through the body, or thinking, or both? Might a deeper exploration of embodied cognition complement the imaginative processes employed by artists working with the body and performance? Can we make the implicit, explicit? How do we make up our minds?

Using neuroscience as a lens, I have undertaken a focused approach to my practice. An enquiry into the neurobiological processes that occur when we imagine, choose and remember[1] has helped me define more specific tools, practices, questions and outcomes, and facilitated a more nuanced and

---

1   In this chapter, I use the terms 'recollect', 'remember' and 'recall' interchangeably. I acknowledge that there is an academic discourse that exists around the semantic interpretations of these words. However, I have chosen not to address these interpretations here for reasons of space.

refined composition process. It has brought an attention to, and uncovering of, the whispering, ghostly fragments of image, feeling and sense that become material, that provide the fodder for performance.

Throughout this chapter I draw on extracts from my research journal (they appear in italics) in order to illustrate specific points. The journal covers a number of performance and research projects that have been implemented whilst undertaking a practice-based PhD. It is written in a range of styles including process descriptions and analyses, commentaries, scripts and texts, academic writings, details of studio sessions and so forth.

I allow my mind's images to course across my consciousness. I wonder why it is that I find it so interesting and comforting to dwell in such a cognitive space. It is surely not nostalgia, for some images are creepy, disturbing, and Not Quite Right. I question them with my conscious mind, now, in the present, interrogating them and the process. Some are just static images, or very short moments or exchanges, a few vivid seconds at most. Do I wish I could have my time again?

I just want to know what I prefer... do images arise first, and then words and gesture follow? And note the language I use about this: the linear expectation of one type of experience following another; the mind's images coursing like the 'anatomical theatre' that Damasio claims is not, in fact, what occurs in the brain when we remember.

It's so easy to return to the habit.

A brief discussion about dualism

The western world still operates squarely within a dualistic model of the mind/body split. René Descartes viewed the world as one divided into physical actions and mental processes. For Descartes, 'thought' and 'the body' are two entirely separate entities. The body is made of material stuff. Reflexive and responsive, the body is regarded as a physical mechanism. The brain is considered part of the body in this context, but the mind and brain are separate. The mind is associated with the soul, and is everlasting and ethereal. All mental processes, thoughts, ideas, imagination and memories occur outside the body. Body and mind are entirely separated into dual realms—the 'dualism' of Cartesian dualism.

Our own experience seems to support this. Doctors and medical personnel, particularly those working in conventional health disciplines, treat physical ailments in the body, and pay scant attention to the patient's mental outlook on his or her illness. We use dualistic frameworks of language about mind and body in our daily lives: we speak of 'the mind's eye', or 'having a good head on one's shoulders'. We wonder 'where we are headed'; we are 'seeing things'; ideas and thoughts 'cross one's mind'. We perceive our thoughts to be physically located in our brain: we rub our foreheads to recall a forgotten memory, and we experience and locate ideas, memories and images in the head, not in other parts of the body.

Such dualistic approaches are often applied in conventional performance techniques too. We might 'embody' an idea, a thought, a feeling, an emotion or an image in rehearsal. We imagine we are wading through honey, or inhabit the breath, shape, gait of an animal in order to manifest character, physical nature, shape or essence. From this we build character, story and narrative. Equally, performance methodologies that are underpinned by physical trainings are often binary in nature, when we let the body 'lead'. In Suzuki training, for example, actors work with physical impulse in order to create dynamic statues in a process that is intended to avoid conscious decision-making about potential physical shape and form. Actors explode into shape from the body's centre in response to an unpredictable and rapid prompt, often a stick whacked on the ground or a short, sharp shout. In this methodology, the body is regarded as the primary generator of material, energy and dynamism. The body is the locus of experience. Nonetheless, it is a dualistic stance, assuming a separation between body and mind.

The head is the vessel for the brain. But my whole body, including my head, is part of my brain.
Today I try to imagine I am just an object in the space. I am no less, or more, important than the floor, a chair, a sound, the light. My body is part of the architecture.
I walk through the space, stop, sway, am still, travel, release.

I do not prioritise spaces in the room, gestures, dwelling spots, attitudes, other objects, light, sound, feelings, senses.
I move, and keep moving, through and with these elements. My body is as objective as these elements. These elements are as important as my body.

The 'body-minded brain': a synthesised approach

In *Descartes' Error: Emotion, Reason and The Human Brain*, neuroscientist Antonio Damasio writes of 'the body-minded brain' as an entity that encompasses mind and body (Damasio, 1994). This is the concept of 'embodied cognition': that there is a finely balanced synthesis between mind (defined as images, imagination, recollection, sensations manifested through neural mechanisms) and the brain, body and environment (Loetscher *et al.*, 2010). In the model of 'the body-minded brain', the organism in its entirety generates responses from and to the environment and itself. The brain processes this reactive and generative information and connectivity by forming neuronal dispositions – what we know as thought. Such a feed-forward, feed-back approach differs greatly from Descartes' hierarchical and linear model. In Damasio's paradigm, images are not located in, or formed by, the brain alone – the brain, the body and the environment are fully involved in the generation of an image. He describes our processes of thought as vast constructions made up of rational thought, memories, emotions and feelings which are managed and monitored by factors inside, or outside, the brain:

> "Sometimes the construction is paced from the world outside the brain, that is, from the world inside our body or around it, with a bit of help from past memory. ...Sometimes the construction is directed entirely from within our brain, by our sweet and silent thought process, from the top down, as it were. That is the case, for instance, when we recall a favourite melody, or recall visual scenes with our eyes closed and covered, whether the scenes are a replaying of a real event or an imagined one." (Damasio, 1994, 97).

This subjective imaginative experience, our sense of ourselves, our thought, our mind, is inextricably bound to brain and body.

My work with EC continues.

Yesterday we recorded a great long conversation about each other – our friendship, what shits us about each other, the nature of love. We talked about the act of not having children, the decision/or not to have them, the reasons this might be, the closing off, the emotional response that provokes in me. I told her about the dream I had, where she really wanted to get married to me and was in a long slim-line white halter neck dress. It was a great conversation. But the audio recorder only worked for three minutes and then ran out of space. We missed it all. We had to try and do it again… and of course it was a completely different, and possibly not as interesting, series of words.

Why do those things happen? Is the chance missed?

There are an infinite number of possibilities.

I am overwhelmed with how much information I have collected, and continue to collect, in this way. It is chaotic, random, rich with imagery and recollection but messy and falling about and flailing.

There are any number of combinations and permutations and ways to go and directions. I must choose. With all my research, I must choose.

I must decide what words to keep and what will never be said out loud.

I must decide what books to read, when to read them, and when to leave them and launch into the writing and the making.

I must decide what information goes into what notebook, and remember to look at it later/be able to find it if/when I need to.

What if I can't find it?

What if the perfect thing was said and I lost it?

Is all this about losing things?

I persevere and persevere with Post-it notes and labels on notebooks and bookmarks and stickers with words on them in books at salient points and categorisation of articles and graphing of movements and recordings of words said out loud and collections of old birthday cards sent from my father to my mother with 'To My Darling Wife' written every time and postcards from Paris in the 50s where they lived for a time.

And I didn't even like them much, really.

As artists and art-makers we are familiar with the notion that highly perceptive and imaginative skills are fundamental to our practice. Sometimes, however, artists are faced with overwhelming choices and challenges in selecting material for inclusion. This is particularly relevant for those working in a devising practice which is self-generating and doesn't rely on external texts or other formal boundaries which frame and contain a piece of work. In my case, adopting a 'body-minded brain' approach to my practice has imbued it with an increased sensitivity to the process of choice in a very helpful way. Exploring such an approach requires a subtle and nuanced shift in emphasis rather than a radical change in practice. It is a re-naming of, and a special interest in, materials and elements that might otherwise have gone unnoticed. It is an approach that acknowledges the exchangeable and interdependent mechanisms that are brought to bear; right there, in the studio, on the floor, listening, articulating and being specific.

Performers adopt many of these exchangeable approaches in tacit ways in their existing practices. In my devising process, I incorporate physical gesture, live recorded monologue, field recordings and personal stories into an integrated piece of live performance. Transcription and re-writing is also used. This is a deeply nuanced activity in which many and varied choices and decisions are made at different moments. Content is often generated and manipulated concurrently, a process that is both exacting and impulsive. I build material by choosing to repeat, sustain or develop a particular idea. For example, I may choose to explore one gesture further, repeating it, extending it, slowing it down, playing with tempo, duration, spatial relationship and so on. Images, texts and movement sequences are gathered and established in this way. Particular expressive moments may resonate or stay with me somehow – I will return to them again and again. I choose them. In essence, I am making decisions in all sorts of ways. Throughout this process I am using my intuition, my body, my impulsive responses, my critical and aesthetic eye, my conscious judgement and my experience to make up my mind.

I walk and walk, am still, play with tempo and architecture and repetition. This sensibility is so different to a completely aimless improvisation.
But I still can't really say why I move here, stay there, or jump up and down over there.
I can't really say why I do it at the time of doing it. Or afterwards. It is just the feeling of it at the time.

Patterns and repetition feel good.
The kinaesthetic feeling of standing with my face one inch from the wall feels
good, especially after the light, airy freedom of moving about in the large space.
Being still feels good after running.
Running feels good sometimes.
Wind in the face feels good. Standing and dropping feels good.

The somatic marker hypothesis: making up my mind

Damasio's 'somatic marker hypothesis' is an example of 'the body-minded brain' in action, and can go some way towards illuminating such a practice of choice.

Damasio describes somatic markers as those momentary physical discomforts when one considers a range of outcomes of a decision and a 'bad feeling' is associated with one of them. The term 'somatic' refers to bodily feeling; the feeling of the body. 'Marker' in this context indicates the feeling that is 'marked' by the image in the mind. We may know somatic markers as 'gut-feelings'.

Damasio acknowledges that there are several rational ways in which we choose between options. Often this occurs in a measured, conscious way. Several courses of action are weighed up and the most logical, or preferable, or beneficial outcome is chosen. Variables such as the ability to delay gratification, benefits that occur now or may arrive later, or urgency of resolution may all be contributing factors to our final decision. Somatic markers occur before any of these conscious decisions are made. When faced with a vast array of options, the somatic marker system gives us a feeling associated with negative outcome. This "allows you to *choose from among fewer alternatives*" (emphasis in the original) (Damasio, 1994:173). Somatic markers, then, are physical short-listing devices produced by 'the body-minded brain' which assist us in making decisions. They are creators of order because they force a preferential system of choosing. Somatic markers do not make the choice for us, but reduce the number of options from which to choose. They "assist in the process of sifting through such a wealth of detail – in effect, reduce the need for sifting because they provide an automated detection of the scenario components which are more likely to be relevant." (*ibid*: 199)

Somatic markers work on an unconscious level and continue to be acquired throughout life. They are the outcome of the internal neural mechanisms that have developed within the brain through evolution – that is, they are part of the brain's 'internal preference system' which is related to survival mechanisms. However, they are also responsive to external circumstances; that is, they are adaptive and change as one's life progresses. They are an example of the remarkable reciprocity between the brain and the body systems.

Shannon Rose Riley provides an eloquent explanation: "Somatic markers are neurological patterns which link a particular recalled image(s) with particular perceptual images, and a particular body feeling... Significantly, somatic markers are not static but become re-marked, re-imagined with every re-collection." (Riley, 2004: 455)

Say I film three takes of myself. Say the first one is a complete open improvisation.
Say the second one is the same but with a specific score using 'Changing the Leading Movement'.
Say the third one explores 'Sustain and Develop'.
Say I observe the first video and make an inventory of customary movement sequences.
Say I use a range of criteria for analysis of my habitual movements: gross or small, high or low or what level, topographic, tempo, propensity for stops and starts, average time between stillness and movement, predominant gaze (intimate, mid-range, eternal), homolateral, homologous, contralateral, symmetrical, favourite plane, etc.
Say I also broaden this to using Laban elements of effort and flow.
Say I plot these elements on a graph.
How would I do that?
This is actually very difficult.
I am not a mathematician, as Mr. Daly who put me in C-stream maths in grade three at Highvale Primary School would attest.
I've done a few diagrams in my sketchbook. I would have to break the movements right down. A graph just portraying frequency of 'gross' movements, for example.
Perhaps it depends on my inventory.

Somatic markers, then, are at work when I am faced with choosing and selecting material from the wealth of detail in my own practice. In this way I make up my mind. My body engages with mind, brain and environment through a unique, complex and profound selection process. When specific images return to my conscious mind, or sounds or gestures resonate, a short-list has already been made. When I choose words to include and words to leave out, I am using my somatic marker system to make an embodied choice.

Such an attentive experience is described succinctly by theatre director Anne Bogart in one of her monthly blog posts:

> "The body constantly receives myriad impressions from multifarious sources, from temperature, visual stimulus, sound, ideas, suggestions, people, odors, colors and so on. But the instantaneous journey of the body's responses to these stimuli is not so simple because the physical sensations are immediately met by and intertwined with your memory, associations, ingrained prejudice, long term goals and learned responses. And in this way, your own body, which is so wrapped up in and ultimately not separate from the world around it, can instantaneously let you know, simply by the level of excitement and energy generated, what needs attention." (Bogart, 2011)

Here is an example of how such an attentive body might select material. I use movement improvisation as a fundamental technique at the commencement of my devising process. This beginning point is often the most open, unbounded and generative stage. I might begin by playing with a gesture, a shape or a simple movement sequence without any text. It may be in response to a theme, an idea, a fragmentary image or a memory. It may not be in response to any theme. At times I score the improvisations, providing a simple structure to work from. Examples of scores are: 'lead from the top of the head' or 'right toe as primary mover' or 'attention to gaze: intimate, middle distance or infinite' or 'be asymmetrical at all times' or 'eyes as limb' or 'reverse impulse'. Sometimes I work in complete darkness for a while. I work with eyes closed, or 'fishtail' – cheat with my eyes open briefly in order to orient myself in space – or move from one state to the other. At times I focus on what feels nice and what is interesting to explore. At other times I attend to patterns that have been/are being created in space. An image may arise following a particular gesture, which I may ignore or respond to. I may become bored, and if I do I work to maintain or re-generate interest. There is a natural propensity here to explore, generate and produce.

At times this stage can be overwhelming and unsatisfying as ideas build and whirl. If, however, I focus attention on my feeling response (read somatic markers), I can sift through the bulk of the material in a way that has affective significance for me. On a practical level, this sometimes is as pragmatic as making a list of gestures/themes/shapes/spaces that have resonated and re-surfaced, and a list of things that didn't. I can repeat this process, sifting again and again, feeling and attending, constantly short-listing to refine my choices. I am left with some sense of a beginning of things, a start, a collation of elements that buzz with interest.

Naming and articulating such material can also provide a place of departure; a place to move away from. I can, for example, choose to explore the ideas that I left out: the duds, the leftovers, and the material that my somatic markers prompted me to avoid. Perhaps this unknown and uncomfortable territory is the juice. What I do know is that when I frame my practice through the 'somatic marker hypothesis', and, more broadly, the concept of the 'body-minded brain', I undertake a particular attention to both form and content in what I make. Such an approach seems to act as a filter for my experience; like a magnifying glass which spans all material but shines a light on that which is remarkable (even if it's unremarkable). As a devisor, this is particularly relevant, because I do not construct performance using scripts, actors and directors in a conventional theatrical sense. Instead I draw on my own experience, memory, imagination and inner life to devise performance that is, ultimately, personal and subjective. There are certainly resemblances in the dynamic energies that often underpin improvisational movement with the automatic response systems that Damasio describes. My particular gestural cadence is the result of evolutionary pressures as well as my unique personal history. Somatic markers could be just as relevant to my movement life as to my everyday life – an embodied collection of my evolutionary history, and an expression of my story so far – my memories, my thoughts, my culture, my personal experiences and my place in the world.

Employing the notion of 'the body-minded brain' as an interpretive framework demystifies the romanticism surrounding the paradigm of 'embodiment'. It provides a pragmatic view of practice, acknowledging it as it changes, grows, and becomes deeper. It doesn't undermine all the physical practices I employ, but upholds and celebrates it as part and parcel of the curious assemblage process that becomes performance. In essence, 'the body-minded brain' is a provocation for devising. Investigating the 'somatic marker hypothesis' has provoked my curiosity about personal memories, stories and narratives, as well as the way I remember things: the importance of articulating images, placements, gestures. Such an investigation validates the method I use, foregrounds the tacit skills I already have, and enlivens my attention to my selective body. With an acknowledgement of these practices I can extend and build on them, explore new approaches for critical reflection, and promote a rigorous and continuing dialogue about the role of the body in making performance.

Kate Hunter is a performance-maker and researcher based in Melbourne, Australia. Her trans-disciplinary work investigates relationships between memory, the body and the brain. She uses recorded and live voice, digital image and performance to investigate remembering, forgetting and imagining. She is the recipient of an Australian Postgraduate Award and Vice Chancellor's Postgraduate Research Award, enabling her to undertake a PhD in Performance Studies at Victoria University, where she is exploring the relationship between memory, neuroscience and performance-making. www.katehuntertheatre.com

Bibliography

Bogart, A. (2011) 'The Body Is A Barometer', *SEE-SITI Extended Ensemble*, available at www.bit.ly/TPbody05

Bogart, A. (2007) *And Then, You Act: Making Art in an Unpredictable World*, New York: Routledge

Bogart, A. (2001) *A Director Prepares: Seven Essays On Art and Theatre*, New York: Routledge

Bogart, A. and Landau, T. (2005) *The Viewpoints Book: A practical guide to Viewpoints and Composition*, New York: Theatre Communications Group

Collins, H. (2010) *Tacit and Explicit Knowledge*, Chicago, IL: University of Chicago Press

Cooper Albright, A. and Gere, D. (eds.) (2003) *Taken By Surprise: A Dance Improvisation Reader*, Middletown, NJ: Wesleyan University Press

Damasio, A. (1999) *The Feeling of What Happens: Body and Emotion in the Making of Consciousness*, San Diego, CA: Harcourt Inc

Damasio, A. (1994) *Descartes' Error: Emotion, Reason and The Human Brain*, New York: Penguin

De Spain, K. (1995) 'A Moving Decision: Notes on the improvising mind', *Contact Quarterly*, 20, 48-50

Govan, E., Nicholson, H. and Normington, K. (2007) *Making a Performance: Devising Histories and Contemporary Practices,* Abingdon: Routledge

Johnson, M. (1987) *The Body in the Mind: The Bodily Basis of Meaning, Imagination and Reason*, Chicago, IL: The University of Chicago Press

Lehrer, J. (2007) *The Decisive Moment: How The Brain Makes Up Its Mind*, Edinburgh: Canongate

Loetscher, T., Bockisch, C.J., Nicholls, M.E.R. and Brugger, P. (2010) 'Eye position predicts what number you have in mind', *Current Biology* 20, 477–572

Riley, S.R. (2004) 'Embodied Perceptual Practices: Towards an Embrained and Embodied Model of Mind for Use in Actor Training and Rehearsal', *Theatre Topics* 14, 445–471

Zarilli, P. B. (ed.) (1995) *Acting (Re)Considered: Theories and practices*, London: Routledge

GLOSSARY

Alexander Technique: F.M. Alexander (1869-1955) was a Tasmanian actor who began to experience chronic laryngitis whenever he performed. He developed a system to re-educate muscle, known as the Alexander Technique. The Alexander Technique embodies a clear set of principles that aim to identify habits and introduce conditions for the psycho-physical training of the actor. These principles provide a framework within which spontaneity and freedom are aligned in a focused, open body and voice, which is fully prepared to respond. It creates a body in a state of alertness and readiness to react - the body and voice of an alive, vibrant, versatile, flexible, physically and emotionally connected performer who is ready to use the appropriate amount of tension for the task in hand.

Authentic Movement was developed by Mary Starks Whitehouse in Los Angeles in the 1940s. Whitehouse had a background as a dancer and later studied Jungian psychoanalysis, devising the Authentic Movement approach based on Jung's method called 'active imagination'. Through bringing attention to movement impulses and expression in a conscious way, the participant tries to uncover insights into the realm of the unconscious. Authentic Movement was developed further by dance therapist Janet Adler who included the idea of the 'witness' in the work. The witness is now a central part of the practice, which can be the therapist or another group member who watches the mover while reflecting on his or her own experience of witnessing the movement. Movers learn to develop an 'internal witness' and reflect on their own movement.

Bardi, Patricia: an American dance artist, choreographer, vocalist and bodywork practitioner based in Amsterdam, where she has been teaching her professional training programme on 'Vocal Dance and Voice Movement Integration' since 1992. A registered Movement Therapist, Patricia Bardi is a founder member of the School for Body-Mind Centering (USA) and Chisenhale Dance Space (London). In 1987 she founded the annual 'Vocal Dance and Theatre Project' in Tuscany.

Active Breath is part of Bardi's 'Vocal Dance' practice. It integrates movement and breath in a variety of ways that can be used as a basis for improvisation. 'Vocal Dance' is a practice that enables the voice to be fully alive and vivid in expression and movement. Besides 'Active Breath', it includes experiential anatomy, sensory awareness and voice, combined with moving in space, and includes improvisation structures combining vocal, physical, visual and temporal elements in solo, duet and group work.

Basic Neurological Patterns: Bonnie Bainbridge-Cohen (2008) describes these patterns as follows: vibration, cellular breathing, sponging and pulsation, navel radiation, mouthing and pre-spinal movement. The twelve vertebrate patterns are based on spinal movement, homologous movement, homolateral movement and contralateral movement. The book has further detailed descriptions of each of the individual patterns. See also Annie Brooks's essay 'Developmental pathways of support' in Wright Miller *et al* (2011: 47-52) where she offers a condensed overview of the dynamics of the patterns tracing a sequence through "yield push reach take hold pull" patterns.

Body-Mind Centering (BMC) was developed in the 1970s in the USA by Bonnie Bainbridge Cohen, a dancer and occupational therapist. The focus of Body-Mind Centering is developing awareness of movement capacity, and also re-patterning where this has been limited. Awareness is brought to the body through breathing, movement, visualisation, touch and study of anatomy. BMC is also called 'experiential anatomy' and works with the body systems including the skin, the skeletal system, the muscular system, the organs, the endocrine system, the nervous system and the fluid system. The practice also includes the investigation of Developmental Movement Patterns, where the participant explores basic underlying movement patterns that begin *in utero* and develop throughout childhood. The patterns include reach and pull, yield and push, homologous, homolateral and contralateral movements, amongst others.

Body-Mind Centering is a registered service mark and BMC is a service mark of Bonnie Bainbridge Cohen.

Corporeal Feminism: Elizabeth Grosz's term for a critical examination of the body and desire that develops understandings of "corporeality, sexuality, and the difference between the sexes...in different terms than those provided by traditional philosophical and feminist understandings" (Grosz, 1994b: vii). Corporeal feminism refigures the body "so that it moves from the periphery to the center of analysis" and foregrounds it as "crucial to understanding woman's psychical and social existence" (*ibid*: ix). For corporeal feminists like Cixous, Butler and others, Grosz maintains that "the body is no longer understood as an ahistorical, biologically given, acultural object. They are concerned with the lived body...[and] tend to be more suspicious of the sex/gender distinction...Instead of seeing sex as an essentialist and gender as a constructionist category, these thinkers are concerned to undermine the dichotomy." (*ibid*: 17-18). Corporeal feminism bridges the gap between feminist theory and queer theory and asserts that it is spurious.

Davis, Joan: a contemporary Irish dancer and choreographer. In the 1970s she founded the first contemporary dance company in Ireland, Dublin Contemporary Dance Theatre, providing access to performances and training. Since 2002, Davis has experimented with integrating somatic practices and contemporary dance, by creating site-specific, interactive performances in an ongoing research project called 'Maya Lila', funded by the Arts Council of Ireland. She also delivers an ISMETA-approved somatic training called Origins at her Co. Wicklow residential centre.

Devising: In their book *Making a Performance: Devising Histories and Contemporary Practices*, Emma Govan, Helen Nicholson and Katie Normington provide a useful overview of the histories and innovations of devised performance across Europe, USA and Australia, drawing on key writers and observers. In their introduction, they attempt a definition, noting that devising does not denote any particular style or methodology, but generally refers to ".. a process of generating a performative or theatrical event often but not always in collaboration with others". They go on to clarify that "the practice of generating, shaping and editing new material into an original performance remains a central dynamic" of a devised process. This is a useful reference; however it should be noted that devising practices can encompass other strategies, such as crafted written text, in addition to practices 'on the floor'.

Embodied Cognition: a field of theories that spans domains such as cognitive psychology, cognitive neuroscience, artificial intelligence and linguistics. It is underpinned by the supposition that the body is connected to every aspect of cognition, including memory, conceptual framing, logical thought, judgement, categories and language. Further, neurologists like Antonio Damasio claim the relationships between body, environment and thought are interdependent and non-hierarchical. Embodied cognition represents a departure from conventional dualistic paradigms in that it acknowledges the crucial and integrated role the body plays in forming thought as well as action. Research in the field is becoming increasingly complex, ranging variously across situated cognition, grounded and bodily states, agency, bodily fragmentation and coherence.

Feldenkrais Method was developed by Moshe Feldenkrais (1904-1984), a physicist, engineer and educator. After injuring his knees and receiving a poor prognosis from physicians, Feldenkrais combined his research into the martial arts, somatic practices, neurology and infant development, creating an approach to learning that promoted self-awareness and improved functioning through the mindful investigation of movement patterns. The method is taught using two related approaches:

Awareness Through Movement: Within an Awareness Through Movement lesson, the Feldenkrais teacher guides students verbally through a (loosely) pre-defined series of movements. The teacher promotes a reflective, mindful engagement with movement in order to develop a clearer self-image. The lessons promote comfort and ease over physical achievement.

Functional Integration: Functional Integration lessons are primarily taught through touch. The Feldenkrais Teacher guides the student through a series of movements, encouraging him to develop strategies for moving with greater ease.

Hay, Deborah: a founder member of Judson Dance Theater, New York, Hay is acknowledged by critics and historians as one of the most relevant and influential representatives of postmodern dance. The Deborah Hay Dance Company's response to the Arts Action Research Team's invitation to define its 'shard-of-a-niche' can be read in full on Hay's website, and gives an insight into Hay's philosophy for dance practice, where 'dance is alive with the recognition of one's perceptual activity'.

SPCP (Solo Performance Commissioning Project), run by Independent Dance, is an opportunity for international dance artists to work intensively with Deborah Hay. Having learned Hay's solo choreographic score, each participant then works towards a solo adaptation over a minimum period of three months daily practice.

Judo: A Japanese martial art involving grappling, throwing and pinning. Based on older traditional forms, Judo was founded in 1882 by Jigoro Kano (1860-1938). Practised competitively, Judo became an Olympic sport at the 1964 Tokyo games.

Kudiyattam is a form of Sanskrit theatre performed in Kerala; it is considered to be the oldest existing Sanskrit theatre in India and also perhaps the oldest extant theatre form in the world. Its origins date back to the 2nd century BCE; thus *Kudiyattam* could easily claim more than 2000 years of continued existence. *Kudiyattam* is performed only in a special temple theatre known as a *Kuthampalam*, literally meaning the 'performance temple', built within the larger temple complex and earmarked exclusively for the performance of *Kudiyattam*. It is performed only by specific communities known as *Chakyar* and *Nambyar*. *Kudiyattam* plays are never completed in a single night. Performance of any single act can take up to eleven nights and the performance of an entire play can take up to 41 nights. Actors write their own performance texts and the daily training sessions, conducted by the guru, typically start in the very early hours of the morning with rigorous physical training led by vocal rendering of the rhythmic syllables. The training period is extensive and it typically takes 6 to 8 years to become an actor.

Laban, Rudolf (1879-1958): a dancer, choreographer and movement theoretician whose work examined dance, pedestrian and industrial applications. He devised his own system of dance/movement notation known as Labanotation or Kinetography Laban.

Laban terms are often used in acting training to define movement styles. As part of his system, Laban identified four basic Effort Elements each with two manifestations: Space (Direct/Indirect), Weight (Light/Strong), Time (Sustained/Quick-Sudden) and Flow (Free/Bound), with eight basic Effort Actions – pressing, punching, wringing, slashing, gliding, dabbing, floating and flicking – each capable of being applied via a combination of the first three effort elements. So 'wringing' could be defined as Direct, Strong, Sustained; 'dabbing' as Indirect, Light, Quick-Sudden.

Natyasastra is the seminal text on Indian Performance Studies, believed to be authored by Bharatha between 200 BCE and 200 CE. Written in Sanskrit, the text contains 6000 verse stanzas in 36 chapters discussing a wide range of issues in theatre arts including dramatic composition, construction of the playhouse, detailed analysis of the musical scales, body movements, various types of acting, directing, division of stage space, costumes, make-up, properties, musical instruments and so on. The aesthetic theory of *rasa* is central to the *Natyasastra*. The term has been widely used in recent debates in aesthetics, philosophy, neuroscience and performance practice as a performative mode generating multiple layers of meaning and experience in artistic practice.

Object Relations theory was developed in Britain by therapists such as W. R. D. Fairbairn, Melanie Klein and D.W. Winnicott from the 1940s onwards. It focuses on the relationships between the client and other 'objects', referring particularly to other people, but also parts of the body, things, and so on. In Object Relations theory, the newly born baby experiences a state of 'merging' with the mother. Over time, the infant begins to develop a sense of separation from 'objects', beginning with the primary relationship with the mother and extending out into the family and, later, society. However, Object Relations continue throughout adult life and we each bring with us a background history that informs our relationships with people, objects and situations.

Ontogenesis describes the process by which an individual organism grows and develops gradually from a simple to a more complex level. It is the developmental journey from our embryonic form towards our full maturity.

Somatics: Somatic practice is an umbrella term for a broad number of body, movement and dance therapies. Physical therapist Thomas Hanna used the term 'somatics' to illustrate his emphasis on the *internal experience* of the client as part of the therapeutic process. In using this term he advocated a balancing of first and third person perspective, rather than a replacing of the one with the other. He critiqued the medical model where a passive patient is examined, diagnosed and treated from the external viewpoint of the therapist, excluding the first-person experience of the patient. Somatic practices tend to include a number of the following elements: emphasis on the internal experience of the mover, body-mind integration, examination of movement habits, development of a larger movement repertoire, and exploration of the relationship between individual and environment.

Taketina was developed by Austrian percussionist Reinhard Flatischler. It is a system of polyrhythmic training and "a musical, meditative group process for people who want to develop their awareness of rhythm... the simultaneity of stabilization and destabilization creates a disturbance that allows participants to repeatedly fall out, and then fall back into rhythm". See www.taketina.com

Bibliography

Bainbridge Cohen, B. (2008) 2nd ed. *Sensing, Feeling, and Action: The Experiential Anatomy of Body-Mind Centering,* Northampton, MA: Contact Editions

Grosz, E. (1994) 'Sexual Difference and the Problem of Essentialism' in Schor and Weed, *The Essential Difference,* Indianapolis, IN: Indiana University Press

Wright Miller, G. *et al.* (2011) *Exploring Body-Mind Centering: An Anthology of Experience and Method,* Berkeley, CA: North Atlantic Books

Also in the series: *Ways of Being a Body*

Volume 1: Nine Ways of Seeing a Body

In the first book in this series, Sandra Reeve succinctly tracks Western approaches to the body from Descartes onwards. The nine ways of seeing a body that she describes are:

~ The body as object ~ The body as subject ~ The phenomenological body ~ The somatic body ~ The contextual body ~ The interdependent body ~ The environmental body ~ The cultural body ~ The ecological body

This admirably short little book has been very widely welcomed as a guide and stimulus for teachers, students and practitioners.

"I love your book and ...I am now using it ... as a text in one of my courses."
Don Hanlon Johnson, Professor of Somatics, California Institute of Integral Studies

"...for anyone who has ever trawled through philosophies of the body it is a welcome relief to have them laid out so clearly.
...essential reading for anyone interested in dance, in movement, in philosophies of the body; for dancers, researchers, students, somatic movement practitioners and for dance movement therapists. Wonderful."
Polly Hudson: Senior Lecturer, Dance Performing Arts, Coventry University

"This book is a delightful, readable set of beginning points or lenses through which to constantly consider and reconsider embodied practice..."
Phillip Zarrilli: Artistic Director, The Llanarth Group

Volume 3: (forthcoming) Body and Awareness

Also from **Triarchy Press:**

A Sardine Street Box of Tricks
Crab Man and Signpost

This is a handbook for anyone who wants to make their own 'mis-guided' tour, walk or walk-performance.

Written by two members of the Exeter-based Wrights & Sites group, the book is based on the mis-guided 'Tour of Sardine Street' that they created for Queen Street in Exeter during 2011.

Designed to help anyone who makes, or would like to make, walk-performances or variations on the guided tour, the book describes a range of different approaches and tactics, and illustrates them with examples from the Queen Street tour. For example:

- Wear something that sets you apart and gives others permission to approach you: "Excuse me, what are you supposed to be?"

- Take a can of abject booze from the street or a momentary juxtaposition of a dove and a plastic bag and mould them, through an action, into an idea

- Attend to the smallest things

- Examine the cracks in your street and the mould on its walls, note its graffiti, collect its detritus, observe how its pavements are used and abused

- Set yourself tasks that passers-by will be intrigued by: they will enjoy interrupting and even joining in with you

- Draw upon ambiguous, ironical or hollowed-out rituals to complement the multiplicity of your walk with intensity of feeling or depth of engagement.

For more information about Triarchy Press, and to buy print and ebooks, please visit our website:
www.triarchypress.net

Lightning Source UK Ltd.
Milton Keynes UK
UKOW050704180613

212445UK00001B/16/P